# BASIC GREEK AND EXEGESIS

## A Practical Manual That Teaches the Fundamentals of Greek and Exegesis, Including the Use of Linguistic Software

## Richard B. Ramsay

PUBLISHING

P.O. BOX 817 • PHILLIPSBURG • NEW JERSEY 08865-0817

Tree image on page 11 © Mark Stay, istockphoto.com; sun image on page 11 © istockphoto.com

Printed in the United States of America

ISBN: 978-1-59638-064-6

## DEDICATION

I would like to dedicate this book to my wife, Angelica,
my best friend and wisest counselor,

the object of my love,
the subject of my joy,
the participle of my life,
past, present, and future.

# CONTENTS

# PREFACE

This practical workbook fills a void in biblical and theological studies, because it prepares the student to do New Testament exegesis, using Greek, but without an extensive knowledge of the language.[1] It integrates the study of Greek with every aspect of exegesis. As the student learns a new step, he also learns the corresponding fundamentals of Greek that enable him to do the exegesis properly. He becomes aware of the importance of using Greek to do serious Bible study, and learns how to use linguistic tools, including recent software. The student studies a biblical text of his or her own choice and prepares a written report on it. He will be surprised at the results of his own research!

In order to do the exercises in this course, the student should purchase or have access to some books, such as *The New Linguistic and Exegetical Key to the Greek New Testament*, by Cleon L. Rogers Jr. and Cleon L. Rogers III (Grand Rapids: Zondervan, 1998), a Greek-English dictionary, and especially a copy of the Greek New Testament. I recommend the latest version of the Greek New Testament sold by United Bible Societies, edited by Kurt Aland and Bruce Metzger, among others. They also sell a version that has a small Greek-English dictionary at the back, which is ideal. If you prefer, you may purchase linguistic software such as *Logos* or *BibleWorks*, which both contain the Greek New Testament, morphological tools, and concordance search tools. *Logos* also sells *A Grammatical Analysis of the Greek New Testament* (which is similar to *The New Linguistic and Exegetical Key*) in electronic form. (The book form is *A Grammatical Analysis of the Greek New Testament*, by Max Zerwick and Mary Grosvenor, 5th ed. [Rome: Biblical Institute Press, 1996].)

I would like to thank the Cuban students from the Los Pinos Seminary, as well as the students from Mérida, Mexico, who took earlier versions of this course in Spanish, as well as a group from Miami International Seminary who went through the English version of the course. They were all very patient with me as I experimented with the first versions of this book. I learned a lot from those first classes that helped me improve the course. Finally, I also want to thank Elliott Green, from Westminster Theological Seminary in Dallas, Texas, for reviewing the book and for giving helpful corrections and suggestions.

There is a free online course based on this textbook. See http://miamiinternationalseminary.com/. First register by clicking on "Create new account." Then log in and find the course called "Basic Greek and Exegesis." The course includes automatically graded quizzes and PowerPoint presentations with audio files that indicate the pronunciation of vocabulary.

---

[1] For those desiring to study a complete course of New Testament Greek, there are many good texts available, such as *Basics of Biblical Greek*, by William D. Mounce, 2nd ed. (Grand Rapids: Zondervan, 2003) or *A New Testament Greek Primer* by S. M. Baugh (Phillipsburg, NJ: P&R, 1995).

# GOALS AND OBJECTIVES

Since this textbook is designed so that it can be used as a course, it is appropriate to mention the goals and objectives:

**Goals**

There are three main goals:
a)  The student will learn the steps of New Testament exegesis.
b)  The student will learn enough fundamentals of New Testament Greek to be able to use linguistic tools and do a serious exegesis.
c)  The student will gain confidence in doing exegesis in the Greek New Testament, and will grow in his or her desire to do serious exegetical study in the preparation of sermons or Bible studies.

**Objectives**

The student will demonstrate that he or she has reached these goals by doing the following:
a)  Write a report of his or her own exegesis of a brief text selected from the New Testament, correctly following the steps studied in the course and using the linguistic tools properly.
b)  Pass an exam on the fundamentals of New Testament Greek, writing the meaning of a list of vocabulary, explaining the meaning of important grammatical terms, identifying noun and verb forms, identifying the function of certain words within their sentences, and translating some Greek sentences to English.

The particular goals and objectives for the lessons are found at the beginning of each lesson.

# LESSON 1

# INTRODUCTION

*In this lesson, you will understand some of the important reasons to study exegesis and Greek. After finishing, you will express your own ideas about these reasons.*

## 1.1 Why study exegesis?

Since every word of the Bible is inspired, we should handle it with extreme care. There is no more sober warning for pastors and teachers than James 3:1–2: "Not many of you should presume to be teachers, my brothers, because you know that we who teach will be judged more strictly. We all stumble in many ways. . . ." This should make us cautious and diligent in our study of the Word.

The work of exegesis is to *draw out* the meaning of the text. It is basically another word for *serious* Bible study. The word comes from the Greek word ἐξάγω (*exágō*), which means literally to "take out, carry out, or lead out." When God inspired each text of the Scriptures, He had a message to communicate, and that is what we want to analyze. We do not want to add our own ideas or draw conclusions that are not expressed in the text, but to *draw out* what is already in the passage. Every time we preach or teach on a biblical text, the listeners should understand clearly that the main point of our message is based on the text. We are teaching the *Word of God*, and not our own ideas.

As we prepare a message or a class, we should apply the following guideline: Suppose someone hears the message and goes home to tell others what it was about. If they ask that person where the idea comes from, or how they could defend such an idea, the person should not hesitate in pointing to the Bible text. There should be no difficulty in demonstrating that the biblical text confirms the main point of the message. For example, if a pastor preaches from Ephesians 2:8–9 (*For it is by grace you have been saved, through faith—and this not from yourselves, it is the gift of God— not by works, so that no one can boast.*), and the main point of his message is that we cannot earn our own salvation, the listener would have no trouble in showing that these verses express that idea. On the other hand, if a preacher's main point is that "faith is believing the impossible," the listener would not be able to demonstrate that idea from the passage. This example is obvious, but actually many pastors and teachers simply think of something they would like to communicate, then they look for some passage to support their own idea. Thus they frequently distort the point of the biblical text.

We should not forget that, as we interpret the Scriptures correctly, guided by the Holy Spirit, we will receive a great spiritual blessing and we will know Jesus Christ better, who is the central message of the Scriptures. Exegesis should never be converted into a mere intellectual exercise. We want to open the Scriptures, just as Jesus did with the disciples on the road to Emmaus, so that our hearts will be warmed.

Luke 24:27, 32
*And beginning with Moses and all the Prophets, he explained to them what was said in all the Scriptures concerning himself. . . .*

*They asked each other, "Were not our hearts burning within us while he talked with us on the road and opened the Scriptures to us?"*

**1.2 Why study Greek?**

For some, learning a foreign language is a fascinating process, because it opens the door to a new world of ideas and customs. However, for others, it means getting lost in a linguistic labyrinth. I recognize that some people are not interested in studying a complete course in Greek. Others simply do not have time to learn a new language. This does not mean that they are not good students, or that they cannot become good pastors, preachers, or teachers.

Nevertheless, I believe that it is very helpful to know enough Greek to do a serious exegesis of a passage of the New Testament. Since the original manuscripts were written in Greek, you really need to know something of the language in order to seek the best interpretation. There are treasures of wisdom waiting to be discovered, but many people lack the tools to find them.

The purpose of this text is to train the student to do a serious analysis of New Testament passages, using a basic knowledge of Greek grammar and of linguistic tools. It teaches the fundamentals of Greek without pretending to provide a mastery of the language, and it also teaches the steps of exegesis. The hope is that the student will become motivated to continue a more complete study of Greek in the future.

**1.3 Examples of the importance of Greek**

There are many things that can be seen only in the Greek text.

**a) Romans 1:17**

For example, Romans 1:17 is difficult to understand in some translations.

*For therein is the righteousness of God revealed from faith to faith: as it is written, the just shall live by faith. (King James Version)*

*For in it the righteousness of God is revealed from faith to faith; as it is written, "But the righteous man shall live by faith." (New American Standard Bible)*

What does the phrase "from faith to faith" mean? At first it sounds nice, but when you think about it, you are not sure what it means. Is it talking about different kinds of faith or about passing the faith from one person to another? There are some loose translations that give totally different interpretations.

*The good news tells how God accepts everyone who has faith, but only those who have faith. It is just as the Scriptures say, "The people God accepts because of their faith will live." (Contemporary English Version)*

*God's way of putting people right shows up in the acts of faith, confirming what Scripture has said all along: "The person in right standing before God by trusting him really lives." (The Message)*

When we look at the Greek text, we find it very helpful. The phrase is ἐκ πίστεως εἰς πίστιν (*ek písteōs eis pístin*). The word ἐκ (*ek*) is a preposition that is normally used to describe movement from inside to outside, for example to explain that someone went *out of* a house.[1] On the other hand, the word εἰς (*eis*) is a preposition that is normally used to describe movement from the outside in, for example, to explain that someone went *into* a house.

---

[1] The word ἐκ can also mean "by means of."

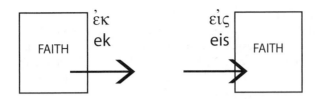

Literally, the text says that righteousness is revealed "out of faith into faith," or "from faith toward faith." As we analyze the words in their normal use, we have a mental image of something: two areas of faith in which the righteousness of God is revealed. The phrase awakens an image of a journey that begins in an area of faith and ends in another area of faith, or possibly the image of a bridge that begins in an area of faith on one end and finishes in another area of faith at the other extreme. While the following is not exactly a literal translation of this verse, the New International Version communicates the idea:

> *For in the gospel a righteousness of God is revealed, a righteousness that is by faith from first to last.*

The New Living Translation, even less literal, shares the interpretation:

> *This Good News tells us how God makes us right in his sight. This is accomplished from start to finish by faith.*

The context of the letter to the Romans supports these two translations. This verse is an introduction to the whole epistle, in which Paul deals especially with the themes of justification and sanctification. Verse 17 is announcing that righteousness comes from God, that it is received initially by faith (in justification), and that it continues to be nourished by faith (in sanctification) throughout life until the end. In other words, justification (righteousness in terms of our legal standing) is by faith, and sanctification (righteousness in terms of our personal walk in holiness) is also by faith, even until we are glorified in the presence of Christ! There is no righteousness that does not come from God by faith.

### b) Cut off or lift up?

In *Secrets of the Vine*,[2] Bruce Wilkinson questions a common translation of a word in John 15:2. He suggests that, instead of saying, "He cuts off every branch in me that does not bear fruit" (NIV), or "Every branch in Me that does not bear fruit, He takes away" (NASB), it should read, "Every branch in me that does not bear fruit, *he lifts up*." The author explains that when a vinekeeper finds a branch that is bent over and buried in the dirt, he often picks it up and shakes off the dust, making it capable of bearing fruit again. He says the word in Greek is αἴρω (*airō*).

If the reader cannot look up the word in a dictionary, he or she will have to accept the author's conclusion. In this case, the lexicon gives several definitions of αἴρω (*airō*): "lift," "take up," "take away," "destroy," "remove." Wilkinson's translation is a valid option, and his arguments are worth considering.[3] The point is not necessarily to solve this problem of interpretation here, but to show that any serious Bible student should at least know the Greek alphabet and know how to look up a word in the dictionary![4]

---

[2] Sister, OR: Multnomah Publishers, 2001.

[3] Verse 6 of the same chapter definitely teaches that branches that are not remaining in Christ will be dried up and cast into the fire. However, verse 2 is speaking of a branch that is in Christ ("in Me").

[4] Another possible interpretation is that being "in Christ" does not necessarily mean being saved, but belonging to the "visible church," that is, making a public profession of faith without truly being born again, such as the case of Judas.

### c) "Full" of the Spirit or "filled" with the Spirit?

One of the most debated theological topics in our day is the meaning of being "filled with the Spirit." There are different interpretations, especially of some passages in Acts. Without trying to resolve all of the issues, I would like to mention some linguistic factors that should help clarify the discussion.

Some try to make technical distinctions between terms such as "baptism of the Spirit," "receiving the Spirit," and "fullness of the Spirit." Nevertheless, when we investigate the use of these phrases in Greek, it is clear that we cannot make such distinctions, because these phrases are used interchangeably. For example, the same event at Pentecost is described with four different phrases: "You will be *baptized* by the Holy Spirit" (1:5), "The Holy Spirit *comes on* you" (1:8), "All of them were *filled* with the Holy Spirit" (2:4), and "I will *pour out* my Spirit on all people" (2:17). Compare also Acts 8:14–18; 10:44–47; and 11:15–16. We must abandon any attempt to make clear technical distinctions between these phrases.

But there is one linguistic distinction that can be noted in Acts, a difference between the adjective "full" and the verb "filled." On the one hand, the author speaks of someone being "full" of the Spirit as a *characteristic* of the person. This describes spiritual maturity. On the other hand, he speaks of someone being "filled" with the Spirit as an *experience*. This describes a special manifestation of the Spirit, enabling the person for a special task. This distinction is confirmed in the Greek.

When the author mentions the *characteristic*, he uses an adjective πλήρης (*plê′rês*, full). This describes a more permanent situation. It is like saying someone is "tall" or "pretty." In these cases, the person is "full" of the Spirit.

Luke utilizes the adjective to describe the men chosen to be deacons in chapter 6 of Acts.

> Acts 6:3
> *Choose seven men from among you who are known to be full [πλήρεις, plê′reis] of the Spirit and wisdom.*

One of the deacons was Stephen, "a man full [πλήρης, *plê′rês*] of faith and the Holy Spirit" (Acts 6:5).

Barnabus was "a good man, full of the Holy Spirit and faith" (Acts 11:24). Here again, the adjective is used, πλήρης (*plê′rês*).

By contrast, when Luke speaks of certain *experiences* in Acts, he uses a *verb* (usually πίμπλημι, *pímplêmi*, but sometimes πληρόω, *plêróō*), normally in passive voice. The passive voice indicates that the subject is receiving the action, such as when we say that a book was "purchased" by someone, or that a house was "painted." In this case, a person is "filled" with the Spirit. This subtle distinction may go unnoticed if we are not careful.

The following passages are examples where the verb is used. Notice that the person filled with the Spirit immediately ministers to others, usually by speaking the Word of God.

> Acts 2:4
> *All of them were filled [ἐπλήσθησαν, eplê′sthêsan, from πίμπλημι, pímplêmi] with the Holy Spirit and began to speak in other tongues as the Spirit enabled them.*

> Acts 4:8
> *Then Peter, filled [πλησθείς, plêstheís, from πίμπλημι, pímplêmi] with the Holy Spirit, said to them . . .*

Acts 4:31

*After they prayed, the place where they were meeting was shaken. And they were all filled* [ἐπλήσθησαν, *eplê´sthêsan*] *with the Holy Spirit and spoke the word of God boldly.*

Acts 9:17–20

*Then Ananias went to the house and entered it. Placing his hands on Saul, he said, "Brother Saul, the Lord—Jesus, who appeared to you on the road as you were coming here—has sent me so that you may see again and be filled* [πλησθῇς, *plêsthê´is*] *with the Holy Spirit." Immediately, something like scales fell from Saul's eyes, and he could see again. He got up and was baptized, and after taking some food, he regained his strength. Saul spent several days with the disciples in Damascus. At once he began to preach in the synagogues that Jesus is the Son of God*

Acts 13:9

*Then Saul, who was also called Paul, filled* [πλησθείς, *plêsthéis*] *with the Holy Spirit, looked straight at Elymas and said . . .*

Acts 13:52–14:1

*And the disciples were filled* [ἐπληροῦντο, *eplêrúnto*, from πληρόω, *plêróō*] *with joy and with the Holy Spirit. At Iconium Paul and Barnabas went as usual into the Jewish synagogue. There they spoke so effectively that a great number of Jews and Gentiles believed.*

The evidence is clear enough to establish a distinction in concepts, based on a distinction in the grammatical forms. The grammatical difference is between adjectives and verbs. The theological distinction is between spiritual maturity as a characteristic of the person and a spiritual experience to prepare a person for a special ministry.[5]

**d) The kingdom of God is "within" you or "among" you?**

Luke 17:21

*Nor will people say, "Here it is," or "There it is," because the kingdom of God is* **within** *you. (NIV)*

*Nor will they say, "Look, here it is!" or "There it is!" For behold, the kingdom of God is* **in your midst**. *(NASB)*

The last clause of this verse has been translated basically two different ways, one represented by the NIV, "within you," and the other represented by the NASB, "in your midst." This makes a significant difference in meaning, and each translation may lead to different theological conclusions. The first translation ("within") may point to inner spiritual renewal as the driving force for changing the world, while the second translation ("in your midst") may point to the importance of interpersonal relationships. Which is correct?

The Greek word ἐντός (*entós*) is found in only one other place in the New Testament, Matthew 23:26. "Blind Pharisees! First clean the *inside* [ἐντός *entós*] of the cup and dish, then the outside also will be clean." However, according to the dictionary, *entós* can mean either "among" or "within."

---

[5] Ephesians 5:18 can also be a confusing verse. It is usually translated, ". . . be filled *with* the Spirit," suggesting that the Spirit is the *content* with which we should be filled. However, some Greek scholars consider that the Greek phrase ἐν πνεύματι (literally "in Spirit") indicates *means* and not *content*, and should be translated, ". . . be filled *by* the Spirit."

Without being dogmatic, I would suggest that in the context of Matthew 23:26, it apparently means "within." Going back to the context of Luke 17:20–21, we see that Jesus was talking about the fact that the kingdom of God was not externally visible ("The kingdom of God is not coming with signs to be observed," verse 20, NASB).

William Hendriksen, in his commentary on the Luke passage, explains that some prefer the translation "among you," because they think Jesus was speaking to the Pharisees, who were not converted, and thus did not have the kingdom of God "within" them. But Hendriksen still prefers the translation "within." He considers that Jesus was speaking generally, saying that the kingdom of God is in peoples' hearts, that He was not speaking exclusively to those who were listening to Him at that moment.

Another commentary, *The Expositors Greek New Testament*, also prefers the translation "within." The commentator argues that this statement is applied to the disciples and not to the Pharisees.

### e) Justification according to Paul and James

One of the most important exegetical dilemmas is the comparison of Paul and James on justification. At first sight, these two authors seem to contradict each other. Compare for example Romans 3:28 (*"For we maintain that a man is justified by faith apart from observing the law."*) with James 2:24 (*"You see that a person is justified by what he does and not by faith alone."*).

However, when we study the various meanings of the word δικαιόω (*dikaióō*) translated in these verses as "justify," we see an important distinction: Paul uses the term in a legal sense, communicating the idea of a divine verdict, while James uses it in the sense of daily life, communicating the idea that a man's righteousness is shown through his deeds.

That is, the Greek word δικαιόω (*dikaióō*) does not always indicate forgiveness of sin or freedom from guilt. In fact, some passages tell us that God Himself is "justified" (Psalm 51:4). Obviously, God does not need forgiveness! In these cases, the idea is that God is *shown to be* righteous. The NIV translates the same verb δικαιόω (*dikaióō*) in James 2:21 as, "Was not our ancestor Abraham *considered righteous* for what he did." For some reason, it does not translate the same verb in the same way a few verses later, in James 2:24, choosing instead to use "justified."

This interpretation fits the context of James better, where he is trying to avoid a misunderstanding. Because James is trying to correct the problem of libertinism, he shows that true faith is manifested through works, through a changed life. However, he certainly is not contradicting Paul's teaching that our legal standing before God is by faith alone.

The reader may or may not agree with these interpretations. However, the purpose of mentioning these passages is to show the importance of learning Greek in order to deal with difficult exegetical problems.

### f) Reading commentaries

Many serious Bible commentaries make reference to Greek words and Greek grammar. The reader who doesn't know anything about the language will be limited in his ability to make use of these resources. For example, William Hendriksen, F. F. Bruce, and John Calvin frequently mention Greek. Many theological books give definitions of Greek words to argue their point or to explain the importance of a grammatical form. If the reader knows nothing of Greek or does not know how to use the proper tools to research the point, he or she will have to blindly accept the author's point of view.

It is a serious thing to stand before a congregation to preach the Word of God, or to explain the Word in a class or Bible study. If we interpret a passage incorrectly, we are distorting what God wants to communicate to His people.

### g) The richness of words

Even when we are studying texts that are not so difficult or polemical, often a study of the words in Greek will enrich our understanding of a passage. For example, when we study the Greek words in John 1:14 (*The Word became flesh and made his dwelling among us. We have seen his glory, the glory of the One and Only, who came from the Father, full of grace and truth.*), we notice that the phrase "made his dwelling" is the translation of a single Greek word that literally means "tabernacled" (ἐσκήνωσεν, eskê′nōsen). This reminds us of the meaning of the tabernacle in the Old Testament and stirs us to think of many ideas and applications. In what sense was the tabernacle a figure of Christ? In what sense did Jesus fulfill the purpose of the tabernacle?

In John 1:1, Jesus is called the "Word." This term in Greek (λόγος, lógos) has an enormous linguistic background. Philosophers would recognize the term, because ancient Greeks had used it frequently. The concept of the "Word" was also important in the Old Testament. However, while taking this background into account, John was using lógos in his own unique way to refer to the revelation of God in Christ.

Terms such as "world" (κόσμος, kósmos), "flesh" (σάρξ, sarx), and "encourage" (παρακαλέω, parakaléō, literally "alongside calling"), are full of meaning, both because of their use in the non-Christian world, and because of their use in the Bible. When we study them, using dictionaries and concordances, we open a treasure chest of meaning.

"Worship" (προσκυνέω, proskunéō) comes from πρός (pros, meaning "toward" or "before") and κυνέω (kunéō, meaning to "kiss"), which suggests the idea of kneeling before someone and kissing his feet. This graphically illustrates the meaning of worship. Whereas some commentators place emphasis on the origin of the English word ("worth" plus "ship") and the consequent implication that worship is a celebration of the *worthiness* of God, the Greek word reminds us of the aspect of *submission* to God.

In John 21:15–17, Jesus asks Peter three times if he loves him. The first two times, Jesus uses the verb ἀγαπάω (agapáō) and Peter answers that he loves him, but he uses another word φιλέω (*philéō*). The third time, Jesus changes the word and uses the same verb that Peter had been using, φιλέω (*philéō*). Throughout centuries, theologians have debated the possible distinction between the Greek words used here. Some consider that Peter used *philéō* because it was somewhat weaker, and that after denying Jesus, he did not dare to say that he loved Jesus with the stronger *agape* love. Then, as they say, Jesus showed His grace, accepted Peter's humble answer by using the same word, and restored him as shepherd of His sheep. Others, and especially more recent scholars, have denied a clear distinction in the meaning of the two verbs, saying that the change was stylistic, possibly to avoid repetition. Whatever your conclusion, the study is fascinating.

**EXERCISE**
Write down the reasons you think it is important to study exegesis and Greek.
(You may choose to write the answers to the exercises on your computer.)

LESSON 2

# THE FUNDAMENTALS OF EXEGESIS

*In this lesson you will learn the four basic steps of exegesis. When you finish, you will practice the first step (analysis of the original context) with a selected Bible text.*

**Introduction**

There are four main steps to exegesis:

> 1) Analyze the original context in which it was written.
> 2) Analyze the linguistic meaning of the text.
> 3) Analyze the biblical and theological implications.
> 4) Apply the message in the present context in which we live.

God revealed His thoughts in a historical context different from ours, and we should bring the same thoughts into our present context. That is, we want to know what He meant to say to the people who received the message originally, and we want to explain it in a way that the people today will understand the same thing.

When we read about the purification of the temple in John 2:13–22, we may wonder why Jesus became so angry. A study of the historical context reveals that the priests had converted the sacrificial system and the whole temple environment into a dishonest business.[1]

The second aspect of exegesis is the linguistic study of the text. What do the words mean? Is there anything special in the structure of the text that helps us understand it? For example, in order to understand John 3:16 better (*For God so loved the world . . .*) we should analyze the meaning of terms such as "world," "only begotten," and "eternal life," as well as the significance of the verb tenses and the way in which the different clauses fit together.

Third, the exegete must consider the theological implications of the passage, seeking to interpret it in the light of the rest of Scripture. The first impression might seem to contradict the teaching of another passage, and he must seek harmony between the two.

Fourth, the work of the preacher and Bible teacher includes the practical application of the message to our lives today. Although the original message of God has not changed, the application may be different for us today. If our message is based on John 2:13–22 (the purification of the temple), we will not speak about being careful how we act around the Jerusalem temple, but probably about how we care for our own hearts and bodies, as well as for the church of Christ (See 1 Corinthians 3:16–17).

---

[1] See for example Alfred Edersheim, *Life and Times of Jesus the Messiah* (Grand Rapids: Eerdmans, 1974), 364–76. Later, updated versions are also available.

# Contextualization

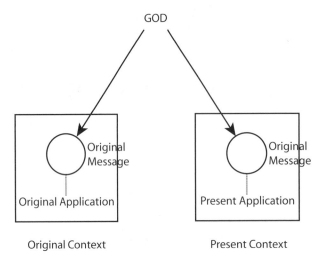

The original message does not change, but the context does change. Contextualization is the process of making a new application of the same message, inserted in the present circumstances. God Himself will guide this process for the benefit of His people.

**The importance of asking questions**

Throughout the whole process of exegesis, it is very important to constantly ask yourself questions. If the exegete doesn't ask questions, he will lose himself in the sea of insignificant data. When the student reflects on the biblical text, his questions orient the study so that he learns new and interesting things. He will probably finish with an application that is more appropriate also, since all of the research was oriented around his concerns.

The Lord guides our study by means of our questions. A pastor or teacher is a messenger for the Lord, and He often puts concerns in our minds so that we will communicate the right message to His people. Many pastors find that when they are struggling with something, many members of their congregations are struggling with something similar. Therefore, when they study a topic that interests them, the fruit of their study will probably benefit the others as well.

Let's consider how to do these four steps. In this lesson we will take a general look at the overall process, and in future lessons we will take a closer look at each step and practice them.

**2.1 Analysis of the original context**

It includes three aspects:
    a) Analysis of the historical context
    b) Analysis of the literary context
    c) Analysis of the context of the history of redemption

**a) The historical context**

To study the historical context, we use encyclopedias, introductions, commentaries, and other articles or books with historical information. We look for data about the times and places related to the passage. If we are studying John 3:16, we look for information about the time of the New Testament, about the apostle John, about Palestine, about the Jewish customs at that time, about the popular philosophies and religions, and about the Roman Empire.

### b) The literary context

One of the most common errors in Bible interpretation is taking a verse out of its context. Serious theological misunderstandings develop this way. You have probably heard the joke about the man who closed his eyes and opened his Bible to whatever page he happened to put his finger on, in order to see what God had to say to him for that day. He first opened to Matthew 23:5, which says, "Then he went away and hanged himself." Next he opened to Luke 10:37, "Go and do likewise!"

In order to understand a text, it is crucial to consider the verses closely surrounding it. Many times, the verse we are studying is directly parallel to, or somehow connected with the previous verses or with the following verses. In the example of Luke 10:37 in the joke above, Jesus is telling the disciples to "go and do likewise" as the Good Samaritan had done, not as Judas had done! We should ask ourselves how our text fits into the section in which it is found.

Furthermore, we should consider the complete book that contains our text. The exegete should familiarize himself with the style of the author, with the principal themes of the book, and with the literary genre. Commentaries and Bible introductions explain general information about a Bible book. For example, if we are studying John 3:16, we will find that the concept of faith is key to the gospel of John (see John 20:31).

Parallel passages are also crucial, especially ones by the same author, or within the gospels. They may open our understanding of the passage we are studying. Many Bibles indicate in the margin or at the bottom of the page the references to corresponding texts.

### c) The context of the history of redemption

This aspect involves reflection about the place of our passage in the plan of salvation. John 3:16 was written after the death and resurrection of Jesus, but it was spoken by Jesus before He died. What does Jesus mean when He speaks of "eternal life"? When does it begin? How will it continue? The exegete must meditate on the global scheme of God's plan. He should always keep in mind the line of history, from beginning to end, with the cross in the center, analyzing how his text fits into the bigger picture. Paul said, "I have resolved to know nothing while I was with you except Jesus Christ and him crucified" (1 Corinthians 2:2). Somehow Jesus is related to every verse in the Bible.

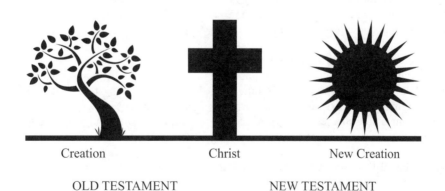

| Creation | Christ | New Creation |
| OLD TESTAMENT | | NEW TESTAMENT |

## 2.2 Analysis of the linguistic meaning

This second step of exegesis is where we will need some knowledge of Greek.

It includes four elements:
a) Study of the textual apparatus (compare variants in manuscripts)
b) Study of semantics (the meaning of the words)
c) Study of morphology (the forms of the words)
d) Study of syntax (structure of the sentences, relationship among the words)

### a) The textual apparatus (variants in the Greek manuscripts)

Most copies of the Greek New Testament include some notes at the bottom of the page regarding different versions that have been found in copies of old manuscripts. This is called the "textual apparatus," and we must include an analysis of these options to do a proper exegesis. Obviously, before we can interpret the meaning of a text, we must determine what the original text was.

If we are studying John 1:4, we will have to consider the different options. One version says (translating from Greek), "in Him *was* life," and another version says, "in Him *is* life." Granted, the difference is not great here, but there are some texts where this analysis can be extremely important.

### b) Semantics (meaning of words)

Words are the basic materials of language and often are used in a wide variety of ways. Since we cannot simply be satisfied with someone else's choice of definitions, we need to research the possible meanings and choose for ourselves the appropriate one for our text. Even if we agree with the translator's choice, we will discover subtle nuances to the words that help us interpret the passage. For John 3:16, we would study the Greek words that have been translated "world," "love," and "believe." For John 1:4 we would study "life" and "light." If we are studying Ephesians 5:23, the meaning of "head" will be key to understanding the role of the husband in the family.

### c) Morphology (the forms of words)

In this process, we analyze the importance of the *forms* of the words: verb tenses, voices, moods, uses of adjectives and nouns. Here we will apply the knowledge of Greek that we will accumulate in this course. The Greek language has very complex and fascinating forms. You will be surprised at the new understanding that will come from this study.

### d) Syntax (structure, relationship between words)

Here we examine how the words fit into phrases and clauses, and how the phrases and clauses relate to each other. We will learn to make a diagram of the sentence, showing these relationships. We will work with the original Greek text, since it was inspired in that language.

The second main step of exegesis, linguistic analysis, culminates in writing your own translation of the text, along with an explanation of why you translated it this way.

## 2.3 Analysis of the biblical and theological implications

There are two aspects of this third step:

a) First, summarize the principal meaning of the text in your own words. There may be many interesting truths and details in the verse, but what is the central point?

b) Then seek to interpret the biblical and theological implications. Sit back and meditate. Try to understand the meaning of the verse in the context of the whole Bible. What are the theological questions that arise? Does your first understanding of the verse seem to contradict another Bible passage? Does it contradict another important doctrine? What does this text teach us about Jesus and salvation? Try to harmonize it with the rest of Scripture.

For example, if you are studying John 3:16, you might have questions such as: If the "world" is all of humanity, and if God loves the "world," why does He not save everybody? If God sent His Son to die for people to have "eternal life," why is not everybody saved? What does it really mean to "believe" in Jesus? What is "eternal life"?

If you are reading certain translations, such as the New American Standard Bible or the King James Version, you might also ask what it means that Jesus was the "only begotten" son. Does this imply that Jesus at some point in eternity did not exist yet? This very phrase actually led to serious doctrinal controversy in the fourth century. Arius and his followers had concluded from statements such as this that Jesus was not fully divine! The subject was debated for years and finally led to the Council of Nicea in 325, in which Arianism was condemned. A better understanding of the meaning of this term could have avoided some severe conflicts!

**2.4 Application in the present context**

Finally, we have not finished our exegesis until we have expressed an appropriate application in our present context and in our own lives. We have not really understood the message until we have applied it concretely to the situation in which we live.

There are two aspects of this step:
a) Reflect on your own context.
b) Find practical applications.

a) First we reflect on our own lives, our families, our church, society in general, currents of popular thought, our community, and our country. If we are studying John 3:16, we might consider what people believe about God, Jesus, and salvation. Why do people need to hear this verse today? How would they interpret it?

b) Then we seek concrete ways to apply what we have learned. For John 3:16, we think of how this verse may encourage us to evangelize others. It may mean we need to grow in our own faith in Jesus. Are we really experiencing "eternal life" now? How can we enjoy our salvation more now? How can we show gratitude for our salvation?

This fourth main step, application, culminates with a brief summary in which we write something like the following:

Since the central message of _____ (Write the Bible reference of text studied.) is

_____ (Write the main message you drafted

previously.), I/we should _____ (Write the main

application.)

**EXERCISES**

**a. Select a text**

The exercises for about half of this textbook will be the research and preparation of an exegesis paper on a passage of your choice. The other exercises practice the fundamentals of Greek.

You will need to buy a notebook to write the results of your research. This may also be done on a computer. At the end of the course, you will write a report that summarizes the most important things you have learned. You will be an expert on the text!

You should now select a text for these exercises. We recommend normally using only one or two verses, because the study will be very complete, and it becomes difficult to analyze an extensive passage. Furthermore, the text should be a verse that is somewhat difficult to understand. This way you will learn to find answers to your questions and discover new teachings. If you think you already understand the verse, you won't learn much. Since John 3:16 and John 1:1 will be used constantly in this textbook, neither of these two verses should be the selected text of study. Ask the Lord to guide you in your selection of a text. When you have decided, write out the verse, using the translation that you normally use for Bible study. The text should be from the New Testament.

Now write down some preliminary questions you have about the verse. What are your doubts? If your verse were John 3:16, maybe you would like to clarify the meaning of the term "world" in this text. In what sense does God "love the world"? Maybe you would want to understand the meaning of "only begotten," "believe," or "eternal life."

**b. Analyze the original context**
In this lesson we will practice the first step of exegesis, analysis of the original context.
1) Analysis of the original context
    a. historical
    b. literary
    c. redemptive

**Questions**
First, you should write down questions regarding these particular areas. These should be your own questions. Don't try to answer the questions yet; just write them down. They will guide your research. Write down your questions about all three aspects:

1) Historical context:

2) Literary context:

3) Redemptive context:

**Research**
Now proceed to do the research:

1) Historical context

a. Read commentaries, introductions, and other books or articles that give information about the historical context.

b. Write down the most important things you find, and possible answers to your questions.

2) Literary context

a. Write down important points from the section in which the verse is found.

b. Observe quickly the whole book in order to get an idea of themes, the general outline, and the literary genre of the book. Write down your observations.

c. Write a brief outline of the book.

d. Write down references and important phrases of parallel passages.

e. Try to answer your questions.

3) Redemptive context

a. Meditate on the plan of redemption and the importance of your text within that plan.

b. Write down your ideas and possible answers to your questions.

# LESSON 3

# THE GREEK ALPHABET

*In this lesson, you will memorize the Greek alphabet, along with the pronunciation and transliteration of each letter. You will also learn about the accents and breathing marks. When you finish, you will be able to write the Greek alphabet, pronounce each letter, and pronounce a list of Greek words.*

The first thing to learn in a language is the alphabet. After this, you can begin to look up words in a dictionary. Fortunately, the Greek alphabet has many visible similarities with English. Furthermore, once you know how to pronounce Greek, you will see many phonetic parallels. For example, we already saw the word κόσμος ("world"). When you know it is pronounced *kósmos*, you see the relation with the English word "cosmos." When you know that ἄνθρωπος ("man") is pronounced *ánthrōpos*, you immediately see the relation with English words such as "anthropology" and "philanthropy." We don't know *exactly* how the ancient Greeks pronounced their language. Nevertheless, we can approximate the pronunciation of the New Testament times.[1]

It is more important to learn the small letters than the capitals, since the Greek New Testament used today is almost completely written in small letters. Even the first word in a sentence begins with a small letter, except when it is also the first word in a paragraph. However, it is a good idea also to recognize the capitals, since they are used for things such as the first word in a paragraph, proper names, and the names of the books of the Bible.

Study the following list of the Greek alphabet. Memorize how to write the letters and how to pronounce them.

---

[1] In the sixteenth century, Erasmus introduced a pronunciation that makes it easier to learn the language, because it makes a clear distinction in sound between all the letters. This has become the most common pronunciation in academic circles and is the one used in this text. The question of pronunciation still stirs debate, since others prefer the pronunciation according to modern Greek. See http://www.biblicalgreek.org/links/pronunciation.html and http://www.elia.org.gr/pages.fds?pagecode=14.02.04&langid=2.

## 3.1 The Greek alphabet

| Small letters | Capitals | Name | Sound |
|---|---|---|---|
| α | Α | alpha | short "a" as in "f<u>a</u>ther" |
| β | Β | beta | "b" as in "<u>b</u>oy" |
| γ | Γ | gamma | "g" as in "<u>g</u>o" |
| δ | Δ | delta | "d" as in "<u>d</u>id" |
| ε | Ε | epsilon | "e" as in "g<u>e</u>t" |
| ζ | Ζ | zeta | "dz" or "ds" as in "a<u>ds</u>" |
| η | Η | eta | long "a" as in "d<u>a</u>te," or "e" as in "h<u>ey</u>!" |
| θ | Θ | theta | "th" as in "<u>th</u>ing" |
| ι | Ι | iota | "i" as in "h<u>i</u>t" or "ee" as in "meet" |
| κ | Κ | kappa | "k" as in "<u>k</u>it" |
| λ | Λ | lambda | "l" as in "<u>l</u>ife" |
| μ | Μ | mu | "m" as in "<u>m</u>other" |
| ν | Ν | nu | "n" as in "<u>n</u>ow" |
| ξ | Ξ | xi | "x" or "xs" as in "e<u>x</u>it" |
| ο | Ο | omicron | short "o" as in "n<u>o</u>t" |
| π | Π | pi | "p" as in "<u>p</u>an" |
| ρ | Ρ | rho | "r" as in "<u>r</u>un" |
| σ, | Σ | sigma | "s" as in "<u>s</u>and" |
| ς | | | The second form, ς, is used when it is the last letter of a word. |
| τ | Τ | tau | "t" as in "<u>t</u>op" |
| υ | Υ | upsilon | "yu" as in "<u>Yu</u>goslavia" or short "i" as in "h<u>i</u>t"[2] |
| φ | Φ | phi | "f" as in "<u>f</u>un," or "ph" as in "<u>ph</u>ilosophy" |
| χ | Χ | chi | "ch" as in German "Ach!" |
| ψ | Ψ | psi | "ps" as in "po<u>ps</u>icle" |
| ω | Ω | omega | long "o" as in "n<u>o</u>te" |

---

[2] Some Greek textbooks recommend using the modern pronunciation of the υ (upsilon), which is an "i" as in "hit." Others prefer to pronounce it as "yu" to distinguish it more easily from the ι (iota). The υ was probably pronounced like "yu" in ancient Greek, and was possibly changed to "i" around the time of the New Testament, but there is no certainty. In these lessons, we will use the pronunciation "yu" to distinguish it from ι (iota). See William Sanford LaSor, *Handbook of New Testament Greek* (Grand Rapids: Eerdmans, 1973).

The vowels are α, ε, η, ι, ο, υ, ω.

If you have access to the Internet, you may observe how the letters are to be drawn at the following site: http://www.inthebeginning.org/ntgreek/alphabet/alpha.htm.[3] (You need to wait a moment for the letters to be drawn.) You may also look at the free online course of Miami International Seminary (MINTS) developed by the author of this text: http://miamiinternationalseminary.com/. First register by clicking on "Create new account." Then log in and find the course called "Basic Greek and Exegesis." You can practice identifying the alphabet with the automatically graded tests, and you can listen to the pronunciation on the PowerPoint presentations. See lesson 2.

### 3.2 Transliteration

To help you pronounce the words correctly, I will normally include a transliteration after the Greek words in these lessons. Since a language is based on its spoken form, it is important to read the Greek words out loud as you do the exercises. Most Greek letters use just one English letter as a transliteration, but some require a combination.

**Transliteration of the Greek alphabet**

| Letter | Transliteration[4] | Name |
|---|---|---|
| α | a | alpha |
| β | b | beta |
| γ | g | gamma |
| δ | d | delta |
| ε | e | epsilon |
| ζ | z | zeta |
| η | ê[5] | eta |
| θ | th[6] | theta |
| ι | i | iota |
| κ | k | kappa |
| λ | l | lambda |
| μ | m | mu |
| ν | n | nu |
| ξ | x | xi |
| ο | o | omicron |
| π | p | pi |
| ρ | r | rho |
| σ, ς | s | sigma |

---

[3] We cannot guarantee that this site will be functioning properly at the moment the student tries to open it.

[4] These are close to the traditional transliterations, but with slight modifications. There are no fixed rules for writing Greek transliterations, and there are a variety of versions. These forms are used in this course to help the student pronounce Greek.

[5] Note that it has a "carrot" (ê) over the letter to indicate that it is a long sound, and to distinguish it from the transliteration of the Greek letter epsilon (ε).

[6] When there are two letters combined, they will be underlined in order to indicate that they represent only one Greek letter (th, xs, yu, ps).

| | | |
|---|---|---|
| τ | t | tau |
| υ | u | upsilon |
| φ | <u>ph</u> | phi |
| χ | <u>ch</u> | chi |
| ψ | <u>ps</u> | psi |
| ω | ō[7] | omega |

Exceptions:

a. The combination of vowels ου is pronounced like "oo," or a long "u." The transliteration of this combination will be written "<u>u</u>" (underlined) to distinguish it from the υ by itself. For example, τοῦτο is pronounced *tú̱to*.

b. When γ is combined with –γ, –κ, or –ξ, the first "g" sound changes to "n." For example, ἄγγελος is pronounced *ángelos* instead of *ággelos*.

c. The combinations of πν and γν are pronounced "n." The π and the γ in these cases are silent. For example, πνεῦμα is pronounced *néuma*,[8] and γνώσομαι is pronounced *nō´somai*.

Read the following words out loud, pronouncing them as indicated by the transliteration:

ἄνθρωπος ("man") is pronounced *án<u>thr</u>ōpos*.

παρακαλέω ("encourage") is pronounced *parakaléō*.

θεός ("God") is pronounced *<u>th</u>eós*.

σάρξ ("flesh") is pronounced *sarx*.

## 3.3 Accents

Accents are used in the Greek New Testament, and in almost any document that quotes Greek. There are three types of accents: acute (ό), circumflex (ô) and grave (ὸ). Originally, these accents indicated musical tone more than emphasis. However, since we do not know exactly how they sounded, we use them now to indicate only emphasis, without making any distinction among the three.

The oldest manuscripts of the New Testament used only capitals, without accents, and without punctuation. The context dictated the meaning where there was ambiguity. The later manuscripts began to use punctuation in the fifth century, then accents in the seventh century, and finally small letters in the tenth century.

For now, it is not worth investing a lot of time to learn how to *write* the accents in Greek. Nevertheless, it is important to learn to *recognize* the accents in order to pronounce the words, and in order to avoid confusion in some cases. Some words have a completely different meaning, depending on the accent. For example, εἰς means "into" whereas εἷς means "one."

Syllables are classified as "ultima" (the last syllable), "penult" (the next to last syllable), and "antepenult" (third from the end).

| antepenult | penult | ultima |
|---|---|---|
| Ἄν– | –θρω– | –πος |

---

[7] Note that it has a line over it to distinguish it from omicron (o).
[8] Some scholars prefer to pronounce the "p."

ἀνθρωπος → sigma

α   η   Th   r   o   p,   Omicron

alpha   nu   theta   rho   Omega

In the case of ἄνθρωπός (*ánthrōpos*, "man"), the accent is over the antepenult. In the case of γινώσκω (*ginō'skō*, "I know"), the accent falls on the penult. And in the case of πιστός (*pistós*, "faithful"), the accent is over the ultima.

### 3.4 General rules of accents

The correct placing of the three accents follows rules that are complex, but for our purposes in this textbook, we will learn only the general rules.

a. The accents in *verbs* try to recede as far back as possible from the ultima, but without going farther than the antepenult.

For example: γινώσκομεν (*ginō'skomen*, "we know"). Here the accent is over the antepenult.

b. The accents in nouns and adjectives try to stay on the same syllable as in their original form, the form that appears in the dictionary (nominative singular, used as the subject of a sentence).

For example: γεωργός (*geōrgós*, "farmer").

c. In a dipthong (combination of two vowels), the Greek accent is over the second vowel, but the word is pronounced as if the accent were over the first vowel.

For example καί is pronounced *kai*, not *ka-í*.

Again, do not worry about writing accents in this course. You only need to learn to recognize them. If you want to learn more about accents, you can study other textbooks.

### 3.5 Breathing marks

If a Greek word begins with a vowel, the first syllable carries what is called a "breathing" mark. There are two kinds of breathing: "rough" (ὁ) and "smooth" (ὀ). Notice that the smooth breathing mark is like an apostrophe, and that the rough breathing mark is like a backwards apostrophe. The rough breathing mark indicates that an "h" sound should be pronounced before the vowel. The smooth breathing does not affect the pronunciation.

If the first syllable is a dipthong (combination of vowels in one syllable), both the accent and the breathing mark are over the second vowel (εἷς), but the word is pronounced as if they were over the first vowel. Practice pronouncing the following words, which begin with a vowel.

ὅτι          *hóti* ("because")

οἶνους       *óinus* ("wine")

εἰ           *ei* ("if")

ἵνα          *hína* ("so that")

Other guidelines: a) The letter ρ at the beginning of a word will also carry a rough breathing mark, and is pronounced like "hr." For example, Ῥωμή ("Rome") is pronounced *Hromé*. b) If a circumflex accent is used in combination with a breathing mark, the circumflex is over the breathing mark (ὧ). c) If an acute or grave accent is used in combination with a breathing mark, the accent is put after the breathing mark (ἄνθρωπος).

### 3.6 Punctuation

Observe the following:

- In Greek, a sentence is normally followed by a period.
- Commas are used generally as they would be in English, to divide clauses or phrases.
- A semicolon (;) is used to indicate a question.
- A period above the line (˙) is the equivalent of a semicolon in English.

### 3.7 Other marks

While they are not common, you need to know some other marks used in the Greek New Testament. The *diaeresis*, which looks like the German umlaut (¨) is sometimes used over an iota to indicate that the letter should be pronounced as a separate syllable from the vowel before it, and not as a dipthong. For example, Ἠσαΐου should be pronounced *Esa-i-u*, and not *Esai-u* (see Matthew 4:14). Also, the student should be aware that, just as in English, Greek sometimes combines two words, drops a letter or two, and puts an apostrophe to replace the missing letter or letters, forming a contraction. In English, for example, *don't* replaces *do not*. In Greek, κἀγώ replaces καί ἐγώ ("and I"). Sometimes the apostrophe is placed at the end of a word, as in μεθ᾽ ἡμῶν which replaces μετά ἡμῶν. This apostrophe appears the same as a smooth breathing mark, but it does not fulfill the same purpose.

### 3.8 Vocabulary

In some lessons, we will study vocabulary that occurs frequently in the New Testament. Practice the pronunciation and memorize the meaning. Sometimes help is given to learn the vocabulary by indicating a word in English that was derived from the Greek. Notice that in a Greek dictionary, the verb forms do not appear in their infinitive form as they would in English. Instead, the verb is listed in first person singular, present tense. For example, instead of ἔχειν (*échein*, "to have"), the word that is listed is ἔχω (*échō*, "I have"). You may listen to the pronunciation of this vocabulary list on the online course of Miami International Seminary. See: http://miamiinternationalseminary.com/. First register by clicking on "Create new account." Then log in and find the course called "Basic Greek and Exegesis." Find lesson 2 and click on the PowerPoint presentations on the vocabulary.

| | |
|---|---|
| ἀγαπάω | (*agapáō*) "I love," "I like." (Among Christians, we speak of "agape" love.) |
| ἀδελφός | (*adelphós*) "brother" (Philadelphia, "city of brotherly love") |
| ἀνήρ | (*anêr*) "man," "husband" (*andr*ophobia, *andr*oid) |
| ἄνθρωπος | (*ánthrōpos*) "man," "human" (phil*anthropy*, *anthropo*logy) |
| γάρ | (*gar*) "because" |
| εἰμί | (*eimí*) "I am" |
| ἔχω | (*échō*) "I have" |
| ἔχει | (*échei*) "he or she has" |
| ζωή | (*zōê'*) "life" (zoology, zoo) |
| θεός | (*theós*) "God" (*theo*logy) |
| ἵνα | (*hína*) "in order that, " "that" |
| κόσμος | (*kósmos*) "world, "order, " "adornment" (cosmos) |
| λέγω | (*légō*) "I say, " "I speak" (diá*léctic*) |
| λέγει | (*légei*) "he or she says, speaks" |
| λόγος | (*lógos*) "word" (dialogue, philology, logic) |

## EXERCISES

Note: After completing the Greek exercises, you may check your answers at the back of the book in "Answers to Exercises."

a. Practice writing the small letters of the alphabet (at least five times each). Memorize the alphabet. Please take time to make sure you can repeat it quickly without errors, both in writing and out loud. If you have access to the Internet, use the following site to learn how to draw the letters: http://www.inthebeginning.org/ntgreek/alphabet/alpha.htm. (Wait a moment for the letters to be drawn.)

| Name | Small letters |
| --- | --- |
| alpha | α |
| beta | β |
| gamma | γ |
| delta | δ |
| epsilon | ε |
| zeta | ζ |
| eta | η |
| theta | θ |
| iota | ι |
| kappa | κ |
| lambda | λ |
| mu | μ |
| nu | ν |
| xi | ξ |
| omicron | ο |
| pi | π |
| rho | ρ |
| sigma, final sigma | σ, ς |
| tau | τ |
| upsilon | υ |
| phi | φ |
| chi | χ |
| psi | ψ |
| omega | ω |

b. Identify these small letters. Write their names and the transliteration.

γ

δ

α

ω

ζ

σ

ς

ρ

τ

φ

ξ

ψ

β

ν

μ

λ

κ

χ

θ

ι

ο

υ

η

ε

π

c. Practice writing the capitals (at least twice each).

| Name | Capital |
|---|---|
| **Name** | **Capital** |
| alpha | Α |
| beta | Β |
| gamma | Γ |
| delta | Δ |
| epsilon | Ε |
| zeta | Ζ |
| eta | Η |
| theta | Θ |
| iota | Ι |
| kappa | Κ |
| lambda | Λ |
| mu | Μ |
| nu | Ν |
| xi | Ξ |
| omicron | Ο |
| pi | Π |
| rho | Ρ |
| sigma | Σ |
| tau | Τ |
| upsilon | Υ |
| phi | Φ |
| chi | Χ |
| psi | Ψ |
| omega | Ω |

d. Identify these capitals. Write their names.

K
Λ
M
N
Σ
P
E
T
Θ
I
Π
A
Δ
B
Φ
Γ
H
Ξ
Z
O
Υ
X
Ψ
Ω

e. Write the meaning of each word. Pronounce each one out loud.

ἀγαπάω
ἀδελφός
ἀνήρ
ἄνθρωπος
γάρ
εἰμί
ἔχω
ἔχει

ζωή
θεός
ἵνα
κόσμος
λέγω
λέγει
λόγος

f. If you have access to the Internet, find the following website and listen to the pronunciation of the phrases from John 1. Find the boxes with the Greek phrases, then click over the box with the mouse, and you will hear the reading. http://www.ibiblio.org/koine/greek/lessons/john1.html.

g. You may also practice identifying the letters of the alphabet and the meaning of the vocabulary on the website of Miami International Seminary (MINTS): http://miamiinternationalseminary.com/. First register by clicking on "Create new account." Then log in and find the course called "Basic Greek and Exegesis." You can practice identifying the alphabet and meaning of vocabulary with the PowerPoint presentations and with the automatically graded quizzes. You can also listen to the pronunciation of the alphabet and the vocabulary on the PowerPoint presentations.

# LESSON 4

# TOOLS FOR LINGUISTIC ANALYSIS

*In this lesson, you will learn how to use some linguistic tools that will be helpful for exegesis. When you finish, you will purchase or gain access to the tools that you will use for studying your selected verse.*

**4.1 Books**

We recommend that you buy, or have on hand, some useful tools for studying the Greek New Testament.

1) First, you need a copy of the Greek New Testament. We suggest that you contact a Christian bookstore, or a seminary bookstore, or go directly to United Bible Societies and ask for the latest version edited by Kurt Aland, Matthew Black, and others, preferably one with a mini-dictionary at the back.

You can find their website at: http://www.biblesociety.org/.

2) One of the most useful tools to study the Greek New Testament is *The New Linguistic and Exegetical Key to the Greek New Testament*, by Cleon L. Rogers Jr. and Cleon L. Rogers III (Grand Rapids: Zondervan, 1998). This excellent book analyzes, verse by verse, most of the more difficult words of the Greek New Testament, giving definitions and explaining forms and grammatical nuances. There is a similar book authorized by the Catholic Church, *A Grammatical Analysis of the Greek New Testament*, by Max Zerwick and Mary Grosvenor, 5th ed. (Rome: Biblical Institute Press, 1996).

3) It is also important to have a Greek-English dictionary or lexicon.

a. Some versions of the Greek New Testament have a small dictionary at the back.
b. Probably the best large lexicon is *A Greek-English Lexicon of the New Testament and Other Early Christian Literature* (BDAG), 3rd ed., rev. and ed. Frederick William Danker, based on the 6th ed. of Walter Bauer's *Griechisch-Deutsches Wörterbuch* (Chicago: University of Chicago Press, 2001).
c. *A Reader's Greek-English Lexicon of the New Testament*, by Sakae Kubo (Grand Rapids: Zondervan, 1975), gives the definitions of Greek words in the same order they are found in the New Testament.
d. The most authoritative and complete dictionary of Greek is the *Theological Dictionary of the New Testament*, ed. Gerhard Kittel, 10 vols. (Grand Rapids: Eerdmans, 1964). This "dictionary" has comprehensive articles on most important words in the New Testament. Not all the authors are conservative theologians, but their articles are valuable because of their linguistic-historical analysis. They explain the use of the words in the Septuagint, in classic Greek, and in the New Testament, author by author.
e. The *Theological Dictionary* mentioned above is also now available in one volume, nicknamed the "Little Kittel": Geoffrey W. Bromily, ed., *Theological Dictionary of the New Testament Abridged in One Volume* (Grand Rapids: Eerdmans, 1985).

f. Another large dictionary for very complete word studies is *The New International Dictionary of New Testament Theology* [NIDNTT ], ed. Colin Brown, 4 vols. (Grand Rapids: Zondervan, 1975, 1986).

4) Complete first-year Greek grammars are also helpful, such as:
    a. *Basics of Biblical Greek*, by William D. Mounce, 2nd ed. (Grand Rapids: Zondervan, 2003).
    b. *A New Testament Greek Primer*, by S. M. Baugh (Phillipsburg, NJ: P&R, 1995).
    c. *Learn to Read New Testament Greek*, by David Alan Black (Nashville: Broadman and Holman, 1994).

5) There are also Greek concordances, such as the *Greek-English Concordance to the New Testament*, by John R. Kohlenberger III, Edward W. Goodrick, and James A. Swanson (Grand Rapids: Zondervan, 1997).

6) Another tool that will identify any form of a word, analyze it, and tell where it is found, is *The New Analytical Greek Lexicon* by Wesley Perschbacher (Peabody, MA: Hendrickson, 1990).

7) Helpful books on textual criticism are:
    a. *New Testament Textual Criticism*, by David Alan Black, ed. (Grand Rapids: Baker, 1994).
    b. *The Text of the New Testament*, by Bruce M. Metzger and Bart D. Erhman, 4th ed. (New York: Oxford University Press, 2005).
    c. *A Textual Commentary of the Greek New Testament*, by Bruce M. Metzger (London: United Bible Societies, 1994). It is organized according to the order of the Bible, made to use along with the Greek New Testament.

You can search the Internet for any of these books, or similar items.

## 4.2 Electronic resources

The number of resources available on the Internet and on CD is expanding too fast to keep up with it. The best thing I can do is recommend a few resources that are available at the moment and suggest that you surf the Web for yourself to find new items. Keep in mind that these websites may be temporarily unavailable, or they may even have been permanently closed since the printing of this book.

1) You may want to use a Greek New Testament online or on CD.
Try *The Greek New Testament* at: http://www-users.cs.york.ac.uk/~fisher/gnt/.
This useful program also gives an analysis of the words at the click of a mouse.

2) Try also another free online *Greek New Testament* at: http://www.greekbible.com/.
The only difference between this and the previous site is that here you must look up one verse at a time.

3) You can also find the Robertson's *New Testament Word Studies* online at:
http://www.godrules.net/wordstudy.html.

4) Find Robertson's *Word Pictures of the New Testament* at:
http://bible1.crosswalk.com/Commentaries/RobertsonsWordPictures/.

5) Greek grammars and courses are available online. Go to the following site to see other recommended sites: http://www.ntgreek.org/other_resources.htm.

6) *Logos Bible Software*
At this moment, I would say that the most complete electronic Bible study program is the *Logos* software, based on the *Libronix Digital Library System*. There are many different versions, beginning with more economical home libraries without Greek. The more scholarly versions contain a large library of books,

including several versions of the Greek New Testament. The program includes maps, dictionaries, concordances, commentaries, and almost everything a pastor would need to do exegesis. Go to http://www.logos.com. This site includes a demo (http://www.logos.com/demo). If you can afford it, I highly recommend considering this software for serious but enjoyable research. I recommend the *Original Languages Library*, the *Scholars Library*, or the *Scholars Library Silver Edition*. I will explain how to use this software in the lessons.

### 7) *BibleWorks*

This is another great program for serious Bible study, which includes more than a hundred different translations, including Greek, Hebrew, German, French, and Latin. The emphasis of this program is concordance work and morphological analysis, but it includes other resources, such as *Nave's Topical Index* and *Robertson's Word Pictures in the New Testament*.

### 8) *Little Greek 101*

This website is a course in basic Greek. We especially recommend listening to the pronunciation of the Greek phrases of John 1: http://www.ibiblio.org/koine/greek/lessons/john1.html.

### 9) *NT Greek*, by Dr. William Ramey

http://www.inthebeginning.org/ntgreek/index.htm.
This website is still being developed, but at the date of this writing, it includes fifteen lessons of a complete first-year course in Greek, with pronunciation, flash card vocabulary exercises, and exercises with answer keys.

### 10) *TekniaGreek (Learn Biblical Greek)*

If you desire to use your computer to write Greek, you need to install a Greek font. I recommend the font called "TekniaGreek." It is free, and it can be found on the following website: http://www.teknia.com. Click on "Free Fonts," "Teknia Greek," "Windows 95–XP" or the appropriate "Macintosh" link, follow the instructions, and the font will install automatically in the proper place on your computer. On the same page you can find a picture of the Greek keyboard so you can learn which letters correspond to the English letters on your keyboard. Find "Download the keyboard layout" and click on "Download the PDF file."

### 11) *MINTS (Miami International Seminary)*

As mentioned previously, you may take advantage of the free resources on the website of Miami International Seminary (MINTS): http://miamiinternationalseminary.com/. This very textbook is the basis for one of their courses designed by the author. First register by clicking on "Create new account." Then log in and find the course called "Basic Greek and Exegesis." This online course includes automatically graded quizzes, a forum, a chat room, and PowerPoint presentations.


## EXERCISE

The exercise for this lesson is simply to investigate the resources mentioned, then purchase or gain access to the ones you would like to use for your exegesis project, whether they are books, software, or Internet resources. You need at least a good copy of the Greek New Testament, a Greek dictionary, and some tool for analyzing morphology, such as *The New Linguistic and Exegetical Key to the Greek New Testament*, or *Logos* software. Write down the tools that you have acquired.

# LESSON 5

# USE OF THE TEXTUAL APPARATUS

*In this lesson, you will learn to use the textual apparatus of the Greek New Testament in order to compare different versions. When you finish, you will investigate the textual apparatus of your selected verse.*

**5.1 Why we use the textual apparatus**

Have you ever wondered why some translations include some phrases or verses that others do not? For example, the King James Version of 1 John 5:7–8 says:

*[7]For there are three that bear record in heaven, the Father, the Word, and the Holy Ghost: and these three are one. [8]And there are three that bear witness in earth, the Spirit, and the water, and the blood: and these three agree in one.*

This could be a very helpful proof text for the doctrine of the Trinity! I quoted this verse to some Jehovah's Witnesses once, and they told me the phrase about the Father, Word, and Holy Spirit was not in the original manuscripts. I assumed that they were wrong about that. They have really been deceived, I thought. However, I went home and began looking at other translations, only to find that most of them do not include this phrase! For example, the NIV reads:

*[7]For there are three that testify: [8]the Spirit, the water and the blood; and the three are in agreement.*

You can imagine how this began to bother me and make me wonder who was really right about the doctrine of the Trinity! Later I realized that there are more than sufficient Bible passages that support the doctrine of the Trinity, even without this verse. But I don't want others to experience the same confusion, and that is why I included this lesson on the textual apparatus.

This is not simply a matter of a different translation of the same Greek words. It is a matter of discovering what the original inspired manuscript said in Greek. After the original documents of the New Testament were written, inspired by the Holy Spirit, many copies have been made. There are more than five thousand copies that contain all or portions of the New Testament. The people who made the copies were very careful, but over the centuries, naturally some errors were introduced. Almost all the errors are insignificant, but some, like the example of 1 John 5:7–8, can be important. In any case, we certainly want to come as close as we can to knowing what the original manuscript said.

Some people are shocked when they first hear about the different versions of the manuscripts. They feel that this undermines their faith in the Bible. Nevertheless, they should not feel so threatened. In the first place, as I already mentioned, the differences among the versions are almost all insignificant, and none of them would change any important doctrine. Most of the variations are like the difference between writing "Jesus" instead of "Christ" or something similar. Second, I believe that God did not permit us to have the original manuscripts because people probably would have worshiped them as religious objects. Finally, although we do not have the original manuscripts, we can trust the Lord that He has left us with trustworthy versions of His Word.

It is like listening to a cassette tape with a message from your father. It is not exactly the same as hearing him in person, and if you make copies of the copies, something of the quality may be lost. In fact, there may be words that you aren't quite sure you understand. Nevertheless, there will be few words that are doubtful, and those details do not change anything important in the message. Furthermore, as his son, you recognize his voice, his way of thinking, and you accept the communication as authoritative, as if you were hearing him in person.

The Greek New Testament has notes at the bottom of the page that explain all the different variations in the Greek manuscripts. These notes are called the "textual apparatus." The study of the textual apparatus is called "textual criticism" or "lower criticism." It is distinguished from "literary criticism" or "higher criticism," which is a study of the development of the original document (author, date, purpose, history of the composition of the document, etc.). On the one hand, "textual criticism" is fairly objective, scientific, and historical. On the other hand, "higher criticism" is less objective and inevitably involves much speculation about how the document may have been composed. In the history of higher criticism, the theologians frequently (but not always) cast doubt on the trustworthiness of the Scriptures.

*Obviously, before any other step in our study of a text, we must make sure which text we are studying! Even before looking up words, we need to know which words to include in the study. This is why the first aspect of our linguistic analysis is to take a look at the textual apparatus.*

**5.2 How to use the textual apparatus**

When you open a New Testament in Greek, you will find notes with symbols at the bottom of the page. For example, on the page of Romans 1:7, I find two notes.[1] The second note, which continues on to the following page, says:

[1] 7 {A} ἐν ῾Ρώμῃ $p^{10, 26vid}$ ℵ A B C $D^{abs1}$ Ψ 6 33 81 104 256 263 424 436 450 1175 1241 1319 1506 1573 1739 1852 1881 $1912^{vid}$ 1962 2127 2200 2464 Byz [K L P] Lect $it^{ar, b, d, (mon) o}$ vg $syr^{p, h, pal}$ $cop^{sa, bo}$ arm eth geo slav $Origen^{gr, lat}$ Chrysostom Theodoret; Ambrosiaster Pelagius Augustine // *omit* (see 1.15) G $it^g$ $Origen^{acc.\ to\ 1739}$

What does this mean? It means that there are different versions of verse 7 in the Greek manuscripts.

This note indicates which manuscripts support which version. Some copies include a phrase, ἐν ῾Ρώμῃ ("in Rome"), and other copies omit the phrase. The explanation of each version, along with the manuscripts that support them are separated by "//."

Among the manuscripts, there are "uncials," "miniscules," and "papyri." The papyri are the oldest manuscripts, and they are represented by the letter p, followed by a number to identify them. They were written on materials made from an Egyptian plant called papyrus. In the example above, one papyrus is mentioned, $p^{10}$. The uncials are documents written only in capital Greek letters. They are not as old as the

---

[1] This is from *The Greek New Testament*, 4th. rev. ed., ed. Kurt Aland, Matthew Black, Carlo Martini, Bruce Metzger, and Allen Wikgren (Stuttgart, Germany: Deutsche Bibelgesellschaft, 2001).

papyri, and are often represented by capital letters such as A, B, C, and D. One uncial is called "Sinaitic," and is represented by the Hebrew letter aleph, א. Others are represented by Greek letters, such as Ψ, Δ, Σ, Φ, etc. Finally, there are other uncials that are not so old, symbolized by numbers that begin with "0," such as 056 and 058 (but none of them are mentioned in the case of Romans 1:7). The "miniscules" are written in small letters and are normally represented by numbers that do not begin with "0" (33, 81, 88, etc.). There are also two miniscules symbolized by the letter $f$, which are called $f^1$ and $f^{13}$ (not mentioned in Romans 1:7).

Some symbols indicate what part of the New Testament is included in the manuscript, as well as other similar details. There are abbreviations that represent groups of documents. For example, "Byz" symbolizes the group of documents called "Byzantine." "Lect" refers to "lectionaries," manuscripts that were used for teaching, and "vg" symbolizes the Vulgate translation in Latin. There are also names of historical figures such as Origen and Augustine, who cited the indicated version in their writings.

In the introduction at the beginning of the Greek New Testament, there should be an explanation of the symbols and manuscripts. Frequently, the Greek New Testament is sold with a little insert that explains the most important symbols, along with the dates of the manuscripts. For a complete study of the documents, see *The Text of the New Testament*, by Bruce M. Metzger and Bart D. Erhman, 4th ed. (New York: Oxford University Press, 2005). There is also an excellent book by Metzger called *A Textual Commentary of the Greek New Testament* (London: United Bible Societies, 1994). It is organized according to the order of the Bible and made to use along with the Greek New Testament.

The most important detail of the textual apparatus for those of us who are not experts in the science of textual criticism, is the letter A, B, C, or D between the braces { }. Don't confuse these letters with the other letters that represent manuscripts, which also include A, B, C, and D, but are not in braces. In the example above, it says "{A}." This letter corresponds to the degree of certainty the experts have in the version that is cited in the Bible text. Letter "A" means they are very certain, letter "B" means there is some doubt, letter "C" suggests considerable doubt, and letter "D" indicates a high degree of doubt. *If you have not carefully studied the science of textual criticism, it is better simply to accept this evaluation of the experts.*

## 5.3 Punctuation notes

On some pages of the Greek New Testament, you will also find notes about punctuation and paragraph breaks. This does not refer to what the experts suggest about the early Greek manuscripts, because they did not have punctuation. Rather, it refers to later copies and translations. For example, on the first page of Romans, you will find notes below the textual apparatus such as:

[a] 1 P: TEV FC VP REB . . .

In the introduction of the Greek New Testament, under the section "The Discourse Segmentation Apparatus,"[2] all of the symbols are explained. In this case, the "P" means that certain translations of the Bible, such as the Today's English Version (TEV) and the Revised English Bible (REB), include a paragraph break where the "a" is found, after verse 1.

## 5.4 Parallel passages

Finally, you might also find references to parallel passages at the bottom of the page of the Greek New Testament. For example, in Romans 1:1, there is a note at the bottom indicating other references ("Ac. 9.15; 13.2; Ga. 1.15") that speak of Paul's calling to preach the gospel.

---

[2] Ibid.

**EXERCISES**

Using the same text you have selected previously, you will do an analysis of the textual apparatus. In your Greek New Testament, examine the textual apparatus at the bottom of the page where your verse is found to see if there are variant readings. If there are, look at the letter in brackets to see how certain the experts are about the version they have used in the Bible text. Don't confuse these letters with the other letters that represent manuscripts, which also include A, B, C, and D, but are not in braces. If you would like to do further research, you can read books such as Metzger and Erhman's *The Text of the New Testament* or Metzger's *A Textual Commentary of the Greek New Testament*. Some serious commentaries such as *The Expositors Greek New Testament* will explain the problem if it is important for the interpretation of the passage. Write down the information about the manuscript variants in your verse, if there are any.

# LESSON 6

# SEMANTICS (PART 1): HOW TO LOOK UP A WORD

*In this lesson, you will learn how to find the meaning of a Greek word. When you finish, you will write the different possible meanings for key words in your study text.*

### 6.1 The use of the dictionary

Remember the example of "cutting off" or "lifting up" (*áirō*) the branch in John 15? When you read a book that mentions a Greek word like this, you need to know how to verify what the author is saying. Many times pastors and authors make mistakes about the meanings of words, often because they think you can simply dissect a word and add together the different meanings of its parts. But that may not be correct. What would happen if you tried to explain the meaning of the word "understand" by taking the literal meaning of each part "under" and "stand"? While the meaning of the word may be related somehow historically to the meaning of its parts, you cannot simply assume that this gives you a valid definition.

Furthermore, words can have a wide variety of meanings. This is true in English as well as Greek. For example, what does the word "tight" mean? It can speak of being in a confined space, or it can also mean "stingy" when referring to the way a person spends his money. It might also be used to show how close friends are. Different authors may use the same word in quite different ways.

If you are studying the difference between Paul and James on their use of the word "justification," you might want to look up the following three words related to righteousness and justification: δίκαιος (*díkaios*), δικαιοσύνη (*dikaiosúnē*), and δικαιόω (*dikaióō*). Once you learn the fundamentals of Greek, you can look up these words for yourself in a dictionary to see the different meanings. Observe what is included in the small dictionary at the back of the fourth Aland edition of the Greek New Testament:

δίκαιος, -α, -ον *conforming to the standard, will, or character of God; upright, righteous, good; just, right, proper; in a right relationship with God; fair, honest; innocent*

δικαιοσύνη, -ης f *what God requires; what is right, righteousness, uprightness, justice; righting wrong; (God's) putting (man) in a right relationship (with Himself); religious duties or acts of charity (Mt 6.1)*

δικαιόω *put into a right relationship (with God); acquit, declare and treat as righteous; show or prove to be right; set free (Ac 13.38; Ro 6.7);* δ. τὸν θεόν *acknowledge God's justice or obey God's righteous demands (Lk 7.29)*

If we look in the larger lexicon by Bauer/Danker (BDAG), each of these words has at least a complete page of information. The meanings given are basically the same as the smaller dictionary, but a multitude of Bible references are given, as well as references to ancient authors and manuscripts. Most names are abbreviated, so you need to look up the meanings of them in a section of abbreviations at the beginning of the lexicon. Complete phrases are quoted in Greek to give the context of the words.

For the verb δικαιόω, four main categories of meaning are listed: 1. "to take up a legal cause, show justice, do justice, take up a cause," 2. "to render a favorable verdict, vindicate," 3. "to cause someone to be released from personal or institutional claims that are no longer to be considered pertinent or valid, make free/pure," and 4. "to demonstrate to be morally right, prove to be right."[1]

You can see how important the study of these words can be. We often think of "justify" only as a technical legal term, but according to the lexicon, this is only one of several uses of the Greek verb δικαιόω. As we saw in the first lesson, we shouldn't impose Paul's use of the word on James.

Another important word to study would be μονογενῆ (*monogenê'*), whose root form is μονογενῆς (*monogenê's*). This is sometimes translated "only begotten," but also as "unique" or "one and only." If you look at several dictionaries and lexicons, you will see that they emphasize the meanings of "unique" or "one and only."

This is the beginning of a study of these words. The purpose here is not to do a complete analysis, but to show how to use the dictionaries.

### 6.2 The use of *The Analytical Greek Lexicon*

Even after studying a lot of Greek, you will still encounter many words that you do not recognize as you read the Greek New Testament. In fact, sometimes you will not even know what the root word is in order to look it up in a dictionary. Suppose, for example, that you are studying John 1:1 in Greek.

Ἐν ἀρχῇ ἦν ὁ λόγος, καὶ ὁ λόγος ἦν πρὸς τὸν θεόν, καὶ θεὸς ἦν ὁ λόγος.
(*En archê' ên ho lógos, kai ho lógos ên pros ton theón, kai theós ên ho lógos.*)

The word ἦν (*ên*), which appears three times in the verse, probably does not appear in your dictionary in that exact form, so you may not know how to look up the meaning. This is where an analytical Greek lexicon can help. You can look up the exact form and find the root form.

For example, under ἦν it will say something like the following:[2]

    3 pers. sing. imperf. (§12 rem. 2) . . . εἰμί

This explains that the root verb is εἰμί (*eimí*). When you look up εἰμί in a dictionary, you see that it means "I am" (or "to be"). Other grammatical points are also mentioned ("3 pers. sing. imperf."), but these will be studied later.

### 6.3 The use of *The New Linguistic and Exegetical Key*

Instead of looking up each unknown word in an analytical lexicon, some prefer to use *The New Linguistic and Exegetical Key*, which follows the order of the New Testament, verse by verse, giving the information for the lesser known words. Suppose you are studying John 3:16:

Οὕτως γὰρ ἠγάπησεν ὁ θεὸς τὸν κόσμον, ὥστε τὸν υἱὸν τὸν μονογενῆ ἔδωκεν, ἵνα πᾶς ὁ πιστεύων εἰς αὐτὸν μὴ ἀπόληται ἀλλ᾽ ἔχῃ ζωὴν αἰώνιον.
(*Hútōs gar êgápêsen ho theós ton kósmon, hō'ste ton huión ton monogenê' édōken, hína pas ho pistéuōn eis autón mê apólêtai al échê zōê'n aiō'nion.*)

---

[1] Frederick William Danker, ed., *A Greek-English Lexicon of the New Testament and Other Early Christian Literature* (BDAG), 3rd ed., rev., based on the 6th ed. of Walter Bauer's *Griechisch-Deutsches Wörterbuch* (Chicago: University of Chicago Press, 2001).
[2] Taken from *The Analytical Greek Lexicon* (London: Samuel Bagster and Sons, 1967). See also Wesley Perschbacher, *The New Analytical Greek Lexicon* (Peabody, MA: Hendrickson, 1990).

You would like to know the meaning of ἠγάπησεν (*êgápêsen*), but this exact form doesn't appear in your dictionary. Let's look at what *The New Linguistic and Exegetical Key* says about the word.

> ἠγάπησεν aor. ind. act. ἀγαπάω (#26) to love (TDNT; TLNT; EDNT; James Moffatt, *Love in the New Testament* [London: Hodder and Stoughton, 1929]; Brown 497 ff; EIM 64–85) Const. aor. viewing all God's individual actions of loving the world as a whole.

This tells us that it comes from ἀγαπάω (*agapáō*), and that it means "to love." (Other grammatical points are also mentioned that we will study later.) Now if you would like to find other definitions of this verb, you can look up ἀγαπάω in a Greek-English dictionary.

### 6.4 The use of software to find the root word

Software such as *BibleWorks* and the online *Greek New Testament* will provide information about root forms. In the online *Greek New Testament*, you can simply click on the mouse over a Greek word, such as ἠγάπησεν and it will tell you the "base form."[3]

| Inflected form: | ἠγάπησεν |
|---|---|
| Base form: | ἀγαπάω |
| Major1: | verb |
| Person: | 3rd |
| Tense: | aorist |
| Voice: | active |
| Mood: | indicative |
| Number: | singular |

*BibleWorks* includes a version of the Greek New Testament called "BibleWorks NT Morphology," that gives the root form plus a grammatical analysis below each word.

> ἠγάπησεν
> ἀγαπάω
> viaa3s

### 6.5 Using *Logos* software dictionaries

In *Logos*, the versions of the Greek New Testament that are best for finding root forms are called *Nestle-Aland Greek NT, 27th Ed. with GRAMCORD* or *Nestlé-Aland Greek New Testament, 27th Edition with McReynolds English Interlinear*. Follow these steps to access these versions (according to version 3.0 of the *Libronix* system):

1. Start at "Home."
2. First, you should set a default Bible version for general use. Click on "customize view," then find "Choose Preferred Bible," and choose your main default Bible version from the scroll-down menu. We

---

[3] http://www-users.cs.york.ac.uk/~fisher/gnt/chapters.html.

recommend an English version for this, such as the New American Standard Bible, 1995 update. Any reference you click on as you read through the dictionaries or commentaries will now pop up in that version. Now scroll down to the bottom of the window and click "Save changes," which will take you back to the home page.

3. Go to "Study Passage." Write in your reference in the box (John 3:16) and click "Go." Another window should open to your passage in the default version.

4. Now you want to temporarily change the Bible version in this window. To do this, click on the icon with two rectangles [⁰/₀] ("Parallel resources") and look at the drop down list. Choose *Nestlé-Aland Greek New Testament, 27ᵗʰ edition with GRAMCORD*. This is probably the second-to-last of the Greek versions on the list. There may be two versions with this name. Make sure to choose the version that includes the translation and the analysis of the form underneath the Greek text. You may prefer a similar version called *Nestlé Aland Greek New Testament 27th Edition with McReynolds English Interlinear*, probably the last on the list of Greek versions. This process will not change the default version that will be used throughout the program. It is only a temporary change.

5. You will see the whole verse you are studying with each word analyzed. For example, in John 3:16, the word ἠγάπησεν appears as follows:

> ἠγάπησεν
> ἀγαπάω
> loved
> VS3AAI (VAAI3S in the McReynolds version)

This tells you the root verb, plus other information that we will study later.

*Logos* software also has several Greek dictionaries available. Follow these steps to find the different meanings of words:

1. Go back to "Home" and practice the first steps again. Write the reference in the box "Study Passage" (in our case, write John 3:16), and click "Go."

2. Under "Other tools," click on "Exegetical Guide."

3. Look at the section called "Word by Word," and find a key word in your passage that you want to study. For example, it might be κόσμον ("world"). Notice that some of the words in the verse may not be listed. If the word you are interested in is not listed, go to the verse in Greek at the top of this window and click on the word. It will then appear below as one of the words to be analyzed.

4. Under your word, you see a brief definition, plus a grammatical analysis (which we will study later), and a list of dictionaries.

5. If you would like to hear the pronunciation of the word, click on the little speaker icon (◀ᶾ ).

6. Click on the name of a dictionary to see the definition.

7. You can also click on "more" to see other resources. You should have *The Theological Dictionary of the New Testament*, but wait until the next lesson to use it.

8. Follow the same procedure for any other key words from your verse.

    If you want to study μονογενῆ (*monogenê´*), you will probably need to click on the word in the verse at the top. Look at some dictionary definitions. Then you might want to click on "more" and look at the *Enhanced Strong's Lexicon*. This tells you that the word comes from two other words, 3441 and 1096. When you click on 3441, it goes to μόνος (*mónos*) which means "alone, . . . only, merely." Click the "back" arrow and then click on 1096. This takes you to γίνομαι (*gínoma*), "to become, to come to pass, to arise, to be made . . .") Some people have associated μονογενῆ with γεννάω (*genáō*, give birth) instead of γίνομαι, and have mistakenly concluded that Jesus did not exist from all eternity, but that at some point he was born into existence. As you study the dictionaries, you realize the meaning has more to do with uniqueness, and does not indicate that Jesus came to exist in some point in time. The term is often used to refer to an "only child."[4] Interestingly, it is used with the word "God" in John 1:18, and obviously refers to Jesus.[5] Again, the linguistic evidence points more to the quality of being the *only one*, and not to a fact of *being born*.

### 6.6 English concordances

If you have absolutely no Greek linguistic tools to work with, you can use *Young's Analytical Concordance* (Eerdmans) or *Strong's Concordance* (Zondervan). In *Young's Concordance*, you can look up the English word in your verse, then find the different Greek words that are translated that way in the King James Version. For example, if you are studying John 3:16, you can look up the English word "love" in *Young's Concordance*. You will find a list of Hebrew words and Greek words that are translated "love," and under each Hebrew and Greek word, a long list of the verses where that word appears. Keep looking until you find John 3:16. It appears under the heading of the Greek word ἀγαπάω. Now that you know the root word, you can look it up in the dictionary.

In *Strong's Concordance* (also based on the King James Version), the verses are not divided into sections according to the Hebrew or Greek word, but are simply listed in biblical order. You can find the word "love," find the verse John 3:16, and note the number for the verb "love" (25). Each number is coded for finding the word in a dictionary at the back. When you look up number 25, you find the verb ἀγαπάω with some definitions.

Some versions of the Bible, such as the New American Standard Bible study edition, include a numbering system that guides you to a dictionary at the back where you can discover the root form of a word. However, even though you can struggle your way through these English tools, it is rather tedious. We recommend learning to use the Greek tools.

### EXERCISES
Using the same text you have selected, continue with the second step of exegesis (linguistic analysis). Now we do step 2.b, the semantic study. Remember: ask yourself questions before you begin.

a. Write down six different English translations of the text. Highlight or underline the differences.

b. Write your verse in Greek.

---

[4] See Luke 7:12; 8:42; 9:38; Hebrews 11:17.
[5] "No one has ever seen God, but God the one and only, who is at the Father's side, has made him known." (NIV)

If you are using a computer, you can type the Greek words using Greek fonts. Your word processor may have a Greek font installed. In that case, you can just change the font from the default (usually Times New Roman or Arial) to the Greek font and begin typing. However, we recommend that you download a free font called "TekniaGreek." Go to the website of "Learn Biblical Greek" http://www.teknia.com/index.php?page=tekniagreek, then find "free fonts," then "TekniaGreek," and choose your type of computer, Macintosh or Windows, then follow the instructions. If you type with a Greek font, you will need to learn how to use the keyboard. Many of the letters are intuitively close to the English letter, but others are not. The TekniaGreek keyboard is shown below. At this point, we recommend not trying to put the accents on, since it can be rather frustrating to find the proper accent.

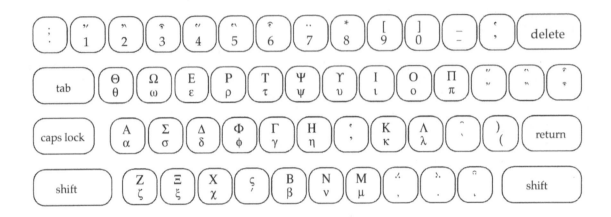

c. Discover the root forms of key words in your text, possibly the words that are translated in different ways. You can use *The Analytical Greek Lexicon*, *The New Linguistic and Exegetical Key*, linguistic software such as *Logos* or *BibleWorks*, *Young's Analytical Concordance*, *Strong's Concordance*, or possibly an English Bible with a numbering system and dictionary.

Write down the "root form" (the "base form") of several key words in your text. If we are studying John 3:16, we find the following key words. The root forms are written in the second column. Some root forms are the same as the form found in the text.

| Form found in John 3:16 | Root form |
| --- | --- |
| οὕτως | οὕτως |
| γάρ | γάρ |
| ἠγάπησεν | ἀγαπάω |
| κόσμον | κόσμος |
| μονογενῆ | μονογενής |
| ἔδωκεν | δίδωμι |
| πιστεύων | πιστεύω |
| ἀπόληται | ἀπόλλυμι |
| ζωὴν | ζωή |
| αἰώνιον | αἰώνιος |

d. Possible definitions

After finding the root forms of the key words, use a dictionary or lexicon to find the different meanings. Write the various meanings of the key words underneath the Greek words. For words that do not seem significant, you may simply write one meaning underneath, according to your favorite translation. We will use John 3:16 as an example.

| Οὕτως | γάρ | ἠγάπησεν | ὁ | θεός | τὸν | κόσμον, | ὥστε | τὸν | υἱὸν | τὸν |
|-------|-----|----------|-----|------|-----|---------|------|-----|------|-----|
| Thus | for | love | (the) | God | the | world | that | the | son | the |
| So | then | long for | | | | world order | | | | |
| Just as | indeed | desire | | | | universe | | | | |
| In this | | | | | | world | | | | |
| way | | | | | | inhabitants | | | | |
| | | | | | | mankind | | | | |
| | | | | | | realm of | | | | |
| | | | | | |   existence | | | | |
| | | | | | | way of life | | | | |
| | | | | | | adornment | | | | |

| μονογενῆ | ἔδωκεν, | ἵνα | πᾶς | ὁ | πιστεύων | εἰς | αὐτὸν | μὴ | ἀπόληται |
|----------|---------|-----|-----|-----|----------|-----|-------|-----|----------|
| only | give | so that | every | the | believe | in | him | not | destroy |
| alone | allow | that | all | | have | | | | kill |
| unique | permit | in | | |   confidence | | | | be lost |
| | place |   order | | | trust | | | | lose |
| | put |   that | | | have faith in | | | | perish |
| | appoint | | | | | | | | be ruined |
| | establish | | | | | | | | die |
| | give out | | | | | | | | pass away |
| | pay | | | | | | | | |
| | produce | | | | | | | | |
| | yield | | | | | | | | |
| | cause | | | | | | | | |
| | entrust | | | | | | | | |
| | grant | | | | | | | | |

| ἀλλ᾽ | ἔχῃ | ζωὴν | αἰώνιον |
|------|-----|------|---------|
| but | have | life | eternal |
| | | | unending |
| | | | everlasting |
| | | | for all time |

Your verse:

e. Questions

Formulate new questions about the possible translations of your text. Note the words whose translations are more doubtful, and whose meanings are more important for understanding the verse.

# LESSON 7

# SEMANTICS (PART 2): HOW TO DO A COMPLETE WORD STUDY

*In this lesson you will learn to do a thorough word study. That is like putting a word under a microscope and examining it carefully. You will find interesting details and subtle nuances. When you finish, you will do a complete word study of several key words or phrases in your selected text.*

To do this study, you need a Greek-English dictionary, possibly a Greek concordance, Kittel's *Theological Dictionary of the New Testament*, or similar electronic resources. You may want to look back at lesson 5 to review the information about these tools. This word study is a continuation of semantics, the second part of the second main step of exegesis:

```
1) Study of the original context
2) Linguistic analysis
      a) textual apparatus
      b) semantics
      c) morphology
      d) syntax
```

A word study begins with the nearest context (surrounding verses, paragraph, chapter, and book) and extends to the larger contexts (books by the same author, then books by other authors). This is like following concentric circles from the smaller center circle to the larger outer circles. The closer to our text, the more helpful the context.

## 7.1 Study of the word in the immediate context

The first task is simply to study the immediate context around the verse. This is fundamental to understanding the meaning of a word. For example, if we are studying John 3:16, and we want to analyze the word κόσμος (world), first we should see how the word is used in the nearby verses. Remember that, according to the dictionary, the possible definitions are: "world," "world order," "universe," "world inhabitants," "mankind," "realm of existence," "way of life," and "adornment."

Let's look at John 3:16–19.

> *For God so loved the **world** that he gave his one and only Son, that whoever believes in him shall not perish but have eternal life. For God did not send his Son into the **world** to condemn the **world**, but to save the **world** through him. Whoever believes in him is not condemned, but whoever does not believe stands condemned already because he has not believed in the name of God's one and only*

*Son. This is the verdict: Light has come into the* **world**, *but men loved darkness instead of light because their deeds were evil.*

When you look at these verses in Greek, you see that each time the word "world" appears in English, the Greek word is κόσμος (or another form of the same word, κόσμον).

What conclusions can we draw from the immediate context about the meaning of this word? First, in these verses it often refers to persons; the "world" can be loved, saved, or condemned. It is difficult to use the possible definitions such as "adornment," "universe," or "way of life" in this context. The only exception might be the phrase about the Son being sent "into the world," which could refer to the physical realm. However, in the same sentence the author refers to the fact that God's intention was not to condemn the world but to save it. Again, the context suggests the meanings of "world" in terms of "mankind" or "world inhabitants."

### 7.2 Study of the lexicon

Now we will investigate the information given in a lexicon. If you do not have access to a Greek-English lexicon, you may skip this and go to the following section. We will use *A Greek-English Lexicon of the New Testament and Other Early Christian Literature* (BDAG).[1] The first thing to do is glance over the article to see if the reference to our text, John 3:16, is mentioned. In fact, we do find it under meaning #5 ("the world, as mankind") section b, which says "of all mankind, but especially of believers, as the object of God's love." Several references are given for this meaning: John 3:16, 17c; John 6:33, 51; John 12:47. Another quick overview shows that the same author, John, is mentioned under several other meanings: #4b "the world as the habitation of mankind" (John, 16:21; 2 John 7; John 12:25), #4c "earth, world in contrast to heaven" (John 6:14; 9:39; 11:27, and many others), and #7 "the world and everything that belongs to it, appears as that which is at enmity with God" (John 1:10; 8:23; 12:25, and many others).

### 7.3 Concordances

A Greek concordance will give you all the passages where the Greek word appears. You can review them to draw your own conclusions about its meaning in each context. If you don't have a Greek concordance, you can also use *Strong's* or *Young's* concordances to find all the places your Greek word appears. This is actually easier with *Young's* because the verses are already grouped according to the Greek word. If you use Strong's, you will have to look for all the verses that have the same code number. A quick review of these verses gives the impression that when John uses the word κόσμος, it has a negative connotation. The verses tell us that the world rejects Jesus, the world does not know him, and that we are not to follow the world.

John 7:7 *The world cannot hate you, but it hates me because I testify that what it does is evil.*

John 17:4 *I have given them your word and the world has hated them, for they are not of the world any more than I am of the world.*

This negative aspect is especially clear in the letters of John. Consider the following verses.

1 John 3:13 *Do not be surprised, my brothers, if the world hates you.*

1 John 5:19 *We know that we are children of God, and that the whole world is under the control of the evil one.*

---

[1] 3rd ed., rev., based on the 6th ed. of Walter Bauer's *Griechisch-Deutsches Wörterbuch* (Chicago: University of Chicago Press, 2001).

The term points to the fallen nature of the world, needing light and salvation, and to the temporal, passing nature of the world. Jesus told the Pharisees that they were of the world, but that He was not. He said His kingdom was not of this world (John 8:23; 18:36).

We should also investigate the way other biblical authors use the word. We find that generally they use it in the same way that John does. James highlights the sinful nature of the "world."

> James 4:4 *You adulterous people, don't you know that friendship with the world is hatred toward God? Anyone who chooses to be a friend of the world becomes an enemy of God.*

Paul makes a contrast between "this world" and the wisdom of God (1 Corinthians 3:19), and teaches that to be in the "world" means to be far from Christ (Ephesians 2:12).

You may need to study a phrase or pair of words from your verse that take on special significance when they are together. For example, if you are studying John 4:23, you may want to study what it means to worship "in Spirit" (ἐν πνεύματι, *en neúmati*) and "in truth" (ἐν ἀληθείᾳ, *en alêthéia*).

### 7.4 *The Theological Dictionary of the New Testament* (edited by Kittel)

This is the most complete lexicon for the study of Greek words. If you have access to these authoritative volumes, you can obtain all the information that you will ever need on important words. There are no fewer than thirty-one pages on the words related to κόσμος. The following summary will give you an idea of the contents of the article.[2]

A. Extrabiblical sources

The article indicates that κόσμος is originally related to the concept of "order" and "adornment." It describes the use of the word by Greek poets and philosophers.

B. The Septuagint (LXX)

In the Septuagint, the word combines the meanings of "order," "adornment," "world," "heavens," and "stars."

C. The New Testament

Kittel's dictionary explains that the New Testament never uses κόσμος in the sense of "order," and that only in one passage is it used as "adornment" (1 Peter 3:3). It distinguishes between several principal senses of the term: 1) the universe, everything created, 2) the inhabited world, the earth, the "theater of history," and 3) humanity, the fallen creation, the "theater of the history of salvation."

The article says that in Paul's letters there is an antithesis between God and the world. "The universe and all the creatures, the visible and invisible world, nature and history, the human and spiritual world, all is united in the same term κόσμος. The κόσμος is the sum of divine creation which has been broken by the fall, which is under the judgment of God. . . . When the κόσμος is redeemed, it ceases to be κόσμος."

The article adds that in the writings of John, the term κόσμος is more fully developed, and that it becomes more precise in its meaning. The concept of κόσμος is in the center of his theology, more than in other writings of the New Testament. The κόσμος is the stage of the drama of redemption. "The history of salvation is a conflict between Christ and the κόσμος."

---

[2] The one-volume abridged version summarizes this article and reduces it to about one-third the size.

As you do a more complete word study, you must be careful to focus on meanings from the New Testament. Finding how writers used a word outside the New Testament may be interesting, but it can also be misleading. To take the meaning of a word from the Greek philosophers, or even from the Septuagint, and apply it to a New Testament context could lead to a serious mistake. For example, the Greek term λόγος (*lógos*, "word") was used by some Greek philosophers to refer to *reason* or to the *rational principle* that governs the universe, which is certainly not the way John uses it in his writings. Of course, the use of a word in the Septuagint may give us helpful background for New Testament usage, but even here we must be careful to avoid a misunderstanding.

### 7.5 Using *BibleWorks* software for complete word studies

*BibleWorks* software contains electronic resources that will help you do a thorough word study and quickly find all the verses in the New Testament that use the Greek word you are investigating. You should use the "search" tool, indicate the version of the Bible you want to search, and write in the word κοσμοσ (*kosmos*); a list will appear with all the verses in the New Testament where the word is used. You can click on each reference, and the corresponding verse will open up. Read the verses to get an idea of how the word is used in that context.

### 7.6 Using *Logos* software for complete word studies

*Logos* software includes many tools for a thorough word study, even a version of Kittel's *Theological Dictionary of the New Testament*. If you have a copy of the software that includes the necessary linguistic tools (such as the *Original Languages Library* or the *Scholar's Library*),[3] you can follow the procedure below to do a Greek word study. (You might also want to watch the *Logos* tutorials that teach how to use their program for a word study.)

1. Go to "Home."
2. Write the reference in the box "Study Passage" (in our case, John 3:16), and click Go.
3. Under "Other Tools," click on "Exegetical Guide."
4. Find the word you wish to study, such as κόσμον.
5. Click on the root word κόσμος. An amazing list of passages will be generated (it may take a few minutes), showing every use of the word in the whole Bible. You can even study the word in the Septuagint. Notice that the verses are grouped according to different forms, such as κόσμον or κόσμῳ. We will explain these different forms in another chapter.
6. The verses are listed in Greek, but if you want to see the English translation, just pass the mouse over the reference, and a little box will open with the whole verse in your default translation.
7. If you want to see more of the immediate context of the particular verse, click on the reference, and the complete passage will appear in another window.
8. If you would like to hear the pronunciation of the word, click on the little speaker icon (◀ ).
9. You may want to look at the article in *The Theological Dictionary of the New Testament*, or in the abridged version of this valuable tool. Just go back to the top of this window and click on the name of the dictionary, and the article will open in another window. If the name of the dictionary does not appear, you may need to click on "more." You will need some time to read the whole article, but you can scroll through and read the most important sections. As mentioned above, it is better to focus on the New Testament and not get distracted or confused with other sources. The closer you can get to the same book or same author, the more likely you are to understand the meaning in your study verse.
10. Try other articles or dictionaries that contain information about your word.
11. Follow the same procedure for any other key words from your verse.

---

[3] http://www.logos.com/.

### 7.7 Drawing a conclusion

After discovering the richness of the word κόσμος, we need to come back to our selected text to see if our study has helped us understand this particular verse. Check your possible translation with the whole text and with the nearby verses to see if your choice produces a contradiction or some other problem. If it does, you will need to reconsider your choice.

For example, you might be studying Matthew 5:31–32. The King James Version reads:

*It hath been said, Whosoever shall **put away** his wife, let him give her a writing of divorcement. But I say unto you, That whosoever shall **put away** his wife, saving for the cause of fornication, causeth her to commit adultery: and whosoever shall marry her that is divorced committeth adultery.*

The New International Version translates:

*It has been said, "Anyone who **divorces** his wife must give her a certificate of divorce." But I tell you that anyone who **divorces** his wife, except for marital unfaithfulness, causes her to become an adulteress, and anyone who marries the divorced woman commits adultery.*

Some people consider that Jesus is talking about *separation* in this text, and others think he is talking about *divorce*. The Greek word is ἀπολύω, which could be translated several different ways, including "put away," "send away," "divorce," "free," or "loose." However, if we translate the word as "separate" or "send away" in the sense of separation only, then we run into a conflict with the latter part of verse 31, which mentions giving a *certificate of divorce*. Furthermore, Jesus is quoting from Deuteronomy 24, where the context is divorce, suggesting that divorce is the topic here also.

After taking into consideration what you have studied, and after taking another look at the context to check for possible contradictions like the example we looked at in Matthew 5:31–32, make your decision about the best way to translate the word you have studied. In the case of John 3:16, we can accept the translation "world," or possibly "mankind" as an alternative. In any case, we now understand that the word often has a negative connotation. We can assume that John 3:16 is suggesting that God loves a *corrupt* mankind, a *fallen* world, a *sinful* humanity. God sent His Son to save a *wicked world*. We gather that the focus is on *quality* more than *quantity*.

**EXERCISES**

a) Select just one or two of the most important words in your chosen text, and do a complete word study, following the explanations and examples in this lesson. Write down your findings and your conclusions about the meaning of the word in your text. You may also need to study a phrase or a pair of words that take on special significance when they are together. Remember that it is not necessary to study every word of your text, but only the most important ones. For example, in John 3:16, it would be especially important to analyze κόσμος (world) or πιστεύω (believe). Neither is it necessary to write down all the information available on the words you study. If the meaning seems clear, it would be better to dedicate your time to another word, or to another aspect of your exegesis.

b) When you finish, write an initial attempt at your own translation of the text. You may want to make this an amplified translation, adding elements that you have learned from your study. Write a brief explanation of why you translated it this way.

# LESSON 8

# MORPHOLOGY (PART 1): NOUNS AND ARTICLES

*In this lesson we begin the study of morphology, the form of words. In particular, you will learn the forms of nouns and articles in Greek. When you finish, you will identify the gender, number, and case of a list of nouns, and you will recognize the use of nouns in some Greek sentences.*

*The student is advised that the next few lessons on Greek grammar will require a serious effort on his or her part. You may need to invest more time on these lessons than you did on the earlier lessons. Please take the time to make sure you understand each section of these lessons. If necessary, read the explanations several times. If you do not know how to do the exercises, go back and study the lesson until you do. Grammar is somewhat like mathematics in that each lesson builds on the previous lesson. If you get lost, go back until you find your way.*

One of the most important passages about the nature of Christ in all of Scripture is John 1:1, "In the beginning was the Word, and the Word was with God, and the Word was God" (KJV, NIV) Unfortunately, some cults have twisted this text and pretend to use it to prove that Jesus was not God, but only "*a god*" among others. Their argument is said to be based on Greek grammar; they say that there is no definite article ("the") before "God" in Greek, and that it should therefore be translated with an indefinite article, "a god." Is this valid? To answer this challenge, we must know something of Greek grammar, especially the use of nouns and articles.

With this lesson, we begin the study of morphology, the form of words. This is the third aspect of the second step of exegesis, linguistic analysis.

---

1) Study of the original context
2) Linguistic analysis
     a) textual apparatus
     b) semantics
     **c) morphology**
     d) syntax

---

First, let's learn a list of vocabulary words.

## 8.1 Vocabulary

Read the following words, using the transliteration to help pronounce them. Practice until you feel sure of the pronunciation. Memorize their meanings. You may also listen to the pronunciation in the online course of Miami International Seminary. See the PowerPoint presentations in lesson 4 at: http://miamiinternationalseminary.com/course/view.php?id=11.

ἀλλά          (*alá*) "but"
βλέπω         (*blépō*) "I see"

| | |
|---|---|
| γῆ | (gê) "earth," "land" (*geo*graphy, *geo*logy) |
| γραφή | (graphê´) "writing" (cali*graph*y) |
| ἐστί | (estí) "it is," "he is," or "she is" |
| ἡμέρα | (hêméra) "day" |
| καί | (kai) "and" |
| κύριος | (kúrios) "Lord" |
| μαθητῆς | (mathêtê´s) "student," "disciple" |
| ὄνομα | (ónoma) "name" |
| ὁ, ἡ, τό | (ho, hê, to) "the" (This is the definite article, which will be studied in this lesson, shown here in masculine, feminine, and neutral genders.) |
| ὅτι | (hóti) "that," "because" |
| πᾶς, πᾶσα, πᾶν | (pas, pasa, pan) "all," "every" (*pan*theism) |
| ποιέω | (poiéō) "I do," "I make" |
| τέκνον | (téknon) "child" |
| υἱός | (huiós) "son" |

## 8.2 Gender and number

A noun is the name of a person, place, thing, or concept. Nouns are classified according to their gender, number, and function in the sentence. In English, while we recognize male and female concepts, there is no grammatical difference in the form of the nouns or articles to indicate their gender. In Greek, there are actually three grammatical genders: masculine, feminine, and neutral.

ὁ ἄνθρωπος, (hó ánthrōpos) "the man" (masculine)

ἡ γῆ, (hê gê) "the earth" (feminine)

τὸ ὄνομα, (tó ónoma) "the name" (neutral)

Notice that all the articles in Greek are different, but they are all translated into English as "the."

The grammatical gender in Greek can be identified by the article. (ὁ = masculine, ἡ = feminine, and τό = neutral). Also, there are certain characteristics of the nouns that indicate their gender. Nouns that end in –ος are normally masculine, nouns that end in –η are normally feminine, and nouns that end in –ον are normally neutral. However, this is just a guideline. There are exceptions, and there are other endings that are ambiguous. Therefore, it is better to judge by the article, and to learn the gender when you learn the vocabulary.

Nouns are also singular or plural. In English, a plural noun is often, but not always, identified by adding an "s" at the end of the word. In Greek, often an iota (ι) is added at the end of the word. Sometimes, other changes indicate plural. The article is again probably the easiest way to recognize the plural. Observe:

| **Singular** | **Plural** |
|---|---|
| ὁ ἄνθρωπος (ho ánthrōpos, "the man") | οἱ ἄνθρωποι (hoi ánthrōpoi, "the men") |
| ἡ γραφή (hê graphê´, "the writing") | αἱ γραφαί (hai graphái, "the writings") |
| ἡ ἡμέρα (hê hêméra, "the day") | αἱ ἡμέραι (hai hêmérai, "the days") |
| τὸ τέκνον (to téknon, "the child") | τὰ τέκνα (ta tékna, "the children") |

## 8.3 The definite article

In Greek, there is a definite article ("the" book), but not an indefinite article ("a" book). When an author wants to express the idea of indefinite in Greek, he may simply leave off the definite article.

ὁ ἄνθρωπος      ἄνθρωπος
the man            a man
(with article = definite)    (without article = indefinite)

However, it is essential to emphasize that the grammatical guideline does not mean that *every time* there is no definite article, the meaning is *indefinite*. An important example of this is John 1:1. The last phrase says καὶ θεὸς ἦν ὁ λόγος (*kai theós ên ho lógos*), which means literally, "and God was the word," and is best translated, "and the Word was God."

As mentioned above, some cults argue that the absence of an article here proves that Jesus was not God, but only "a god." Nevertheless, there is no linguistic basis for this. In fact, in the very same verse, John 1:1, there is another noun without an article that has the meaning of a definite noun. It says ἐν ἀρχῇ (*en archê*) without the article. But the best translation is "in *the* beginning." The context forces us to translate it that way. After all, what would it mean to say, "In a beginning . . ."? Another example is 1 Thessalonians 4:15, where neither "word" (λόγῳ, *lógō*) nor "Lord" (κυρίου, *kuríu*) has an article before it, but the natural way to translate this is, "For this we say unto you by *the* word of *the* Lord" (KJV).

When the normal order of words is inverted (not "the word was God," but instead literally "God was the word") the first word is often without an article. This order puts more emphasis precisely on the fact that the Word was *God*.[1] A grammatical rule called "Colwell's rule" states: "Definite predicate nouns which precede the verb usually lack the article."[2]

Finally, some linguists have noticed a grammatical subtlety in this verse that indicates why it was necessary for John to express himself this way to avoid confusion. In *Word Pictures*, Robertson says:

> By exact and careful language John denied Sabellianism by not saying *ho theos een ho logos*. That would mean that all of God was expressed in *ho logos* and the terms would be interchangeable, each having the article. The subject is made plain by the article, *ho logos*, and the predicate without it, *Theos*, just as in John 4:24 *pneuma ho Theos* can only mean "God is spirit," not "spirit is God."[3]

Sabellius, third century A.D., held a position called "modalism," which sustains that God exists in three different forms, but that there are not three persons in the same Godhead who exist at the same time. You need to understand some Greek grammar in order to benefit from these commentaries and linguistic observations. You might also appreciate the fact that a misunderstanding of the grammar in this text could open the door to a heretical understanding of the Trinity!

## 8.4 Proper names

In Greek, proper names (John, Peter, Mary) may have an article, or they can be without the article, but they never have an indefinite meaning. For example, Πέτρος (*Pétros*) means "Peter" and not "a Peter." When a proper name has a definite article in Greek, it is translated without an article. For example, Matthew 1:2 says,

---

[1] Roberto Hanna, *Grammatical Aid to the Greek New Testament* (Grand Rapids: Baker, 1983), John 1:1.
[2] David P. Wallace, *Greek Grammar Beyond the Basics* (Grand Rapids: Zondervan, 1997), 257–67
[3] A. T. Robertson, *A. Robertson's Word Pictures in Six Volumes* (electronic ed.), *Logos* software.

Ἀβραὰμ ἐγέννησεν τὸν Ἰσαάκ
(*Abraám egénnêsen ton Isaák*)

The article is τὸν. Literally, it says, "Abraham gave birth to **the** Isaac," but it should be translated, "Abraham gave birth to Isaac."

In other words, in Greek a proper noun may have an article or not have an article, but it never has the sense of indefinite. On the other hand, in English, a proper noun never uses any kind of article, definite or indefinite. (It is not correct to say either "a Peter" or "the Peter").

## 8.5 Subject, verb, direct object, and indirect object

A simple sentence has only one subject and one verb. A subject does something, and the verb describes what the subject does or what the subject is. The subject and the verb make up the nucleus of the sentence. We will use "S" to indicate the subject and "V" to indicate the verb.

The man speaks.<br>(S)   (V)

The following diagram also shows the use of the words. There are different ways to make sentence diagrams, but in this textbook, we will use a vertical line that passes through the underlined words to indicate the subject and verb:

The man | speaks.<br>(S)     (V)

Frequently a sentence includes a direct object that receives the action of the verb.

The man sees the brother.<br>(DO)

We will use a vertical line just touching the horizontal line and an arrow to indicate a direct object ( _|→ ).[4]

The diagram is as follows:

The man | sees |→ the brother.<br>(S)     (V)     (DO)

Many times there is also an *indirect object* (IO), which receives an indirect effect of the action.

The man bought *me* a book.

In this case, the book received the direct action of the verb "bought," and I received the indirect action. That is, the book was bought, but it was bought *for me*.

---

[4] The traditional symbol is simply the vertical line touching the horizontal line ( _|_ ), but I add the arrow to illustrate the effect of the verb on the direct object.

The diagram looks like this:

```
                    (IO)
                    me
                   /
  The man | bought |→ a book
   (S)       (V)      (DO)
```

In the diagrams in this book, we will use a slash " / " above the verb to indicate an indirect object.

**8.6 Cases**

In English, *nouns* maintain their form, no matter what their use in the sentence. That is, we can say, "A brother has a son," or "A son has a brother," without changing the nouns "son" and "brother." On the other hand, some *pronouns* do in fact change their form to indicate their use. For example, we say, "*I* see the man," but "The man sees *me*." "I" is the form for the subject of a sentence, and "me" is the form for a direct object.

In Greek, all nouns and pronouns are modified to show their use. This permits changing the order of the words without confusing the reader. The different uses of the nouns are called "cases." There are five cases in Greek. We will use the same noun, "brother" (ἀδελφός) in all of the following examples:

a. *Nominative*—when the noun is used as a subject.

ὁ ἀδελφὸς βλέπει τὸν υἱόν.
(*ho adelphós blépei ton huión.*)
The brother sees the son.

b. *Genitive*—when the noun is used to express possession.

ὁ ἄνθρωπος βλέπει τὸν υἱὸν τοῦ ἀδελφοῦ.
(*ho ánthrōpos blépei ton huión tu adelphú.*)
The man sees the son of the brother.

c. *Dative*—when the noun is used as an indirect object.

ὁ ἄνθρωπος λέγει λόγον τῷ ἀδελφῷ.
(*ho ánthrōpos légei lógon tō adelphō.*)
The man says a word to the brother.

d. *Accusative*—when the noun is used as a direct object.

ὁ υἱὸς βλέπει τὸν ἀδελφόν.
(*ho huiós blépei ton adelphón.*)
The son sees the brother.

e. *Vocative*—when a person is spoken to directly.

ὁ ἄνθρωπος λέγει λόγον, ἀδελφέ.
(*ho ánthrōpos légei lógon, adelphé.*)
The man speaks (or says) a word, Brother.

### 8.7 The declension of the article

As mentioned above, the article is the best sign of case, gender, and number of a noun. The following table demonstrates the forms of the article in all cases (except vocative) and genders, singular and plural. This list of forms is called the "declension" of the article.

**Singular**

| Case | Masculine | Feminine | Neutral |
|---|---|---|---|
| Nominative (the) | ὁ (ho) | ἡ (hê) | τό (to) |
| Genitive (of the) | τοῦ (tu) | τῆς (tês) | τοῦ (tu) |
| Dative (for the, to the) | τῷ (tō) | τῇ (tê) | τῷ (tō) |
| Accusative (the) | τόν (ton) | τήν (tên) | τό (to) |

**Plural**

| Case | Masculine | Feminine | Neutral |
|---|---|---|---|
| Nominative | οἱ (hoi) | αἱ (hai) | τά (ta) |
| Genitive | τῶν (tōn) | τῶν (tōn) | τῶν (tōn) |
| Dative | τοῖς (tois) | ταῖς (tais) | τοῖς (tois) |
| Accusative | τούς (tus) | τάς (tas) | τά (ta) |

Note that the forms of dative singular have a small iota (ι) under the letters (ῳ and ῃ). This is called the "iota subscript," and it does not change the pronunciation of the letter.

### 8.8 The declension of some nouns

The following table shows the forms of some nouns in all their cases, in singular and plural, accompanied by the article. The list of forms of a noun is called the "declension" of the noun. Remember that the translation in English will not express the gender or the case with any change in the form of the noun, but it may use a phrase to express the case, such as "of" or "for."

ὁ ἀδελφός (*ho adelphós*) the brother

| Case | | Transliteration | Translation |
|---|---|---|---|
| SINGULAR | | | |
| Nominative | ὁ ἀδελφός | (*ho adelphós*) | the brother |
| Genitive | τοῦ ἀδελφοῦ | (*tu adelphú*) | of the brother |
| Dative | τῷ ἀδελφῷ | (*tō adelphō´*) | for the brother |
| Accusative | τὸν ἀδελφόν | (*ton adelphón*) | the brother |
| Vocative | — ἀδελφέ | (*adelphé*) | Brother! |
| | | | |
| PLURAL | | | |
| Nominative | οἱ ἀδελφοί | (*hoi adelphói*) | the brothers |
| Genitive | τῶν ἀδελφῶν | (*tōn adelphō´n*) | of the brothers |
| Dative | τοῖς ἀδελφοῖς | (*tois adelphóis*) | for the brothers |
| Accusative | τοὺς ἀδελφούς | (*tus adelphu´s*) | the brothers |
| Vocative | — ἀδελφοί | (*adelphói*) | Brothers! |

τὸ τέκνον (*to téknon*) the child

| SING. | | | |
|---|---|---|---|
| N. | τὸ τέκνον | (*to téknon*) | the child |
| G. | τοῦ τέκνου | (*tu téknu*) | of the child |
| D. | τῷ τέκνῳ | (*tō téknō*) | for the child |
| A. | τὸ τέκνον | (*to téknon*) | the child |
| V. | — τέκνον | (*téknon*) | Child! |
| | | | |
| PL. | | | |
| N. | τὰ τέκνα | (*ta tékna*) | the children |
| G. | τῶν τέκνων | (*tōn téknōn*) | of the children |
| D. | τοῖς τέκνοις | (*tois téknois*) | for the children |
| A. | τὰ τέκνα | (*ta tékna*) | the children |
| V. | — τέκνα | (*tékna*) | Children! |

ἡ γραφή (*hê graphê*) the writing

| SING. | | | |
|---|---|---|---|
| N. | ἡ γραφή | (*hê graphê´*) | the writing |
| G. | τῆς γραφῆς | (*tês graphê´s*) | of the writing |
| D. | τῇ γραφῇ | (*tê graphê´*) | for the writing |
| A. | τὴν γραφήν | (*tên graphê´n*) | the writing |
| V. | — γραφή | (*graphê´*) | Writing! |

**PL.**

| | | | |
|---|---|---|---|
| N. | αἱ γραφαί | (*hai graphái*) | the writings |
| G. | τῶν γραφῶν | (*tōn graphō´n*) | of the writings |
| D. | ταῖς γραφαῖς | (*tais grapháis*) | for the writings |
| A. | τὰς γραφάς | (*tas graphás*) | the writings |
| V. | — γραφαί | (*graphái*) | Writings! |

Some nouns contain irregularities. When you encounter a form that you do not recognize, you should look in the appendix, or in a dictionary to see if it is similar to another word whose forms you recognize. Normally the article and the context will help to identify the case, gender, and number of the nouns.

### 8.9 τὸν κόσμον

If you read John 3:16 in Greek, you will see that the noun κόσμος takes on a different form; it ends in –ν (κόσμον).

Οὕτως γὰρ ἠγάπησεν ὁ θεὸς τὸν κόσμον
(*Hútôs gar êgápêsen ho theós ton kósmon.*)
For God so loved the world . . .

Notice that the phrase τὸν κόσμον is similar to τὸν ἀδελφόν. We can suppose that τὸν κόσμον is the masculine accusative singular form of ὁ κόσμος. We can also deduce that the phrase is the direct object of "loved."

If you are using linguistic software, you may find something like the following analysis of the word κόσμον found in John 3:16.[5]

| Inflected form: | κόσμον |
|---|---|
| Base form: | κόσμος |
| Major1: | noun |
| Case: | accusative |
| Number: | singular |
| Gender: | masculine |

Now we can understand these explanations. When we speak of the "inflected" form, we simply mean that it is a modification of the base form. The inflected form gives us clues to the grammatical use of the word. The table confirms what we have discovered:

- "Major1" is simply the category, showing what kind of word it is, such as noun, verb, or preposition.
- "Accusative" case indicates that the word is used as a direct object.
- The chart also confirms that the noun is masculine in gender and singular in number.

---

[5] Greek New Testament, http://www-users.cs.york.ac.uk/~fisher/cgi-bin/gnt?id=0403, (Nov. 10, 2004).

### 8.10 The predicate nominative

When a noun is used after a form of the verb "to be," it is called a predicate nominative (PrNom).

> The man **is** a <u>brother</u>.
> (PrNom)

In Greek, the predicate nominative is in the nominative case. The verb "to be" in Greek is εἰμί (*eimí*, "I am"). In third person singular, the verb is ἐστί (*estí*: "it, he, or she is"). The forms of this verb can be found in the appendix.

> ὁ ἄνθρωπος ἐστὶ ἀδελφός.
> (*ho ánthrōpos estí adelphós.*)
> The man is a <u>brother</u>.

We will use the equals symbol ("=") to indicate a predicate nominative. The diagram is like this:

> <u>ὁ ἄνθρωπος</u> | ἐστὶ = <u>ἀδελφός</u>.

> <u>The man</u> | is = <u>a brother</u>.

Matthew 16:16 contains an example of a predicate nominative. Peter confesses to Jesus, "You are the Christ." "You" ( Σὺ) is the subject, "are" (εἶ) is the verb, and "the Christ" (ὁ Χριστὸς) is the predicate nominative.

> Σὺ εἶ ὁ Χριστὸς.
> (*Su ei ho Christós.*)
> You are the Christ.

The diagram is like this:

> <u>Σὺ</u> | εἶ = <u>ὁ Χριστὸς</u>

> <u>You</u> | are = <u>the Christ</u>

### 8.11 Recognizing the forms

It is difficult to memorize all the possible forms of the nouns. Therefore, you need to learn to *recognize* the indicators of gender, number, and case. They are not always obvious, but there are several clues that help. The most obvious forms are for the genitive and dative cases. If you see a noun that ends in –ων, you can be sure that it is genitive plural. (The ending –ων can also be a participle, a verb form that we will study later. However, if it is a *noun*, it is genitive plural.) If you see a noun that ends with –ου, you can be sure that it is genitive singular. If you find a noun that ends in –ῳ, or –ῃ, you can be sure that it is dative singular. Here the clue is the iota subscript. ( ). If you encounter a noun that ends in –οις, or –αις, you know that it is dative plural. For other nouns, you need to look at the article to be sure. For example, when you see ὁ —ος , and οἱ —οι, you know that they must be nominative singular and plural, respectively. When you see the combinations τὸν —ον, and τοὺς —ους, you know they are accusative singular and plural. The letters η and α normally indicate feminine gender, with the exception of nominative neutral and accusative plural (τὰ τέκνα).

Even though it is not necessary to memorize all the forms, it would be very helpful to know at least the forms of the definite article, since it indicates the gender, case, and number of the noun that it precedes. Memorize these forms:

**THE DEFINITE ARTICLE**

| CASE SING. | Masc. | Fem. | Neutral |
|---|---|---|---|
| N. | ὁ | ἡ | τό |
| G. | τοῦ | τῆς | τοῦ |
| D. | τῷ | τῇ | τῷ |
| A. | τόν | τήν | τό |
| PL. | | | |
| N. | οἱ | αἱ | τά |
| G. | τῶν | τῶν | τῶν |
| D. | τοῖς | ταῖς | τοῖς |
| A. | τούς | τάς | τά |

**8.12 Using *Logos* software to analyze nouns**

The steps for finding the form of a Greek noun in *Logos* software are the following:

Option 1
1. Start at "Home."
2. Write in your reference in the box "Study Passage" and click "Go."
3. Under "Other Tools" click on "Exegetical Guide."
4. Find the noun you want to analyze, such as κόσμον.
5. Notice under the word the root form and several definitions: "κόσμος: *universe, earth, world system, people, adorning, adornment, tremendous amount.*"
6. You can also read the explanation of the form. It says "Noun, Masculine, Singular, Accusative."
8. Look also at the other nouns in your verse.
9. Finally, you can click on the sound icon and listen to the pronunciation.

Option 2
1. Use the first two steps above.
2. Go to the Bible version in the other window that should be open to the text and change the Bible version to *Nestlé-Aland Greek New Testament, 27ᵗʰ edition with GRAMCORD*, or to the *Nestlé-Aland Greek NT with McReynolds Interlinear*. To do this, click on the icon with the two rectangles, find the version, and select it.
3. You will see the whole verse you are studying with each word analyzed. For example, just as we mentioned at the beginning of the lesson, the term "world" shows the following:

κόσμον
κόσμος
world
NMSA (NASM in the McReynolds version)

4. Point to the word you are interested in, right click the mouse, and select "Display information." An information window will open that explains the meaning of the letters NMSA and gives information on the word.

5. If you leave the information window open, you can pass the mouse over other words in the Greek text, and the information automatically changes to the newly selected word.

**EXERCISES**

a. Write the forms of the definite article in Greek.

Singular

|  | Masculine | Feminine | Neutral |
|---|---|---|---|
| nominative |  |  |  |
| genitive |  |  |  |
| dative |  |  |  |
| accusative |  |  |  |

Plural

|  | Masculine | Feminine | Neutral |
|---|---|---|---|
| nominative |  |  |  |
| genitive |  |  |  |
| dative |  |  |  |
| accusative |  |  |  |

b. Write the principal use of each case:

nominative case

genitive case

dative case

accusative case

vocative case

c. Identify the gender, number, and case of the following nouns. (In some cases there may be more than one possibility.) Try to find clues in the articles, but if you are not sure, look up the words in the tables of section 3.8.

|  | Gender | Number | Case |
|---|---|---|---|
| οἱ ἀδελφοί |  |  |  |
| τοῦ ἀδελφοῦ |  |  |  |
| τῶν ἀδελφῶν |  |  |  |
| τὸ τέκνον |  |  |  |
| τὰ τέκνα |  |  |  |
| τοῖς τέκνοις |  |  |  |
| τῇ γραφῇ |  |  |  |
| τῶν γραφῶν |  |  |  |
| ταῖς γραφαῖς |  |  |  |
| τῆς γραφῆς |  |  |  |

d. Write the meaning of the following words:

ἀλλά

βλέπω

γῆ

γραφή

ἐστί

ἡμέρα

καί

κύριος

μαθητής

ὄνομα

ὁ, ἡ, τό

ὅτι

πᾶς, πᾶσα, πᾶν

ποιέω

τέκνον

υἱός

e. 1) Identify the use of the words or phrases in the following sentences (both English and Greek). Put an "S" below a subject, "V" below a verb, "DO" below a direct object, "IO" under an indirect object, "PrNom" below a predicate nominative, and "Poss" under a noun or phrase in its possessive form. 2) Indicate the case of each noun in the Greek sentences (Nom, Accus, Dat, Gen). 3) Translate the Greek sentences into English.

1) The teacher sees the student.

2) The student has a book.

3) The teacher bought me a book.

4) The student is the brother of the man.

5) The student read the book to the teacher.

6) The brother is the teacher of the child.

7) ὁ ἄνθρωπος ἔχει ἀδελφόν.

8) ὁ ἀδελφὸς λέγει λόγον.

9) ὁ ἄνθρωπος λέγει λόγον τῷ ἀδελφῷ.

10) ὁ ἀδελφός ἐστιν ὁ μαθητῆς.

11) τὸν ἄνθρωπον βλέπει ὁ κύριος.

12) βλέπω τὸ τέκνον τοῦ ἀδελφοῦ.

13) τὴν γραφὴν ποίει ὁ υἱός.

14) ὁ ἀδελφὸς ἔχει τὴν γραφὴν τοῦ κυρίου.

15) τῷ τέκνῳ λέγει λόγον ὁ κύριος.

16) ὁ υἱὸς λέγει ὄνομα τῷ ἀδελφῷ.

17) τῷ ἀδελφῷ λέγει ὄνομα ὁ υἱός.

f. Make a diagram of the following sentences.

1) ὁ ἄνθρωπος ἔχει ἀδελφόν.

2) ὁ ἀδελφός ἐστιν ὁ μαθητῆς.

g. Find the nouns and the verbs in your Greek study text. Use the verse you have already written in Greek. Identify the use of the nouns. Put an "S" below a subject, "V" below a verb, "DO" below a direct object, "IO" under an indirect object, "PrNom" below a predicate nominative, and "Poss" under a noun or phrase in its possessive form. You might need the help of a Greek dictionary, *The New Linguistic and Exegetical Key*, an analytical lexicon, or linguistic software.

# LESSON 9

# MORPHOLOGY (PART 2): ADJECTIVES, ADVERBS, PRONOUNS, AND PREPOSITIONS

*In this lesson, you will continue to study the morphology of Greek words, focusing now on adjectives, adverbs, pronouns, and prepositions. When you finish, you will identify the adjectives, adverbs, pronouns, and prepositions in some sample sentences in both English and Greek, as well as in your own study verse.*

It is important to recognize the use of these words, just as we saw in the analysis of the meaning of *ek* and *eis* in Romans 1:17, and just as we saw in the study of being "full" of the Spirit ("full" as an adjective versus "filled" as a verb) in the book of Acts.

As another example, suppose you are reading a commentary on John 1:1 that mentions the grammatical importance of the preposition in the phrase, "the word was *with* God" (πρὸς τὸν θεόν, *pros ton theón*). *Robertson's Word Pictures* says the following:

> Though existing eternally with God, the Word was in perfect fellowship with God. *Pros* with the accusative presents a plane of equality and intimacy, face to face with each other.[1]

Why does he mention that the Greek word *pros* (πρὸς) has a certain meaning with the accusative? This is one of the grammatical points we will study in this chapter.

First, let's learn some new vocabulary.

## 9.1 Vocabulary

Learn this list of vocabulary. Pronounce these words over and over, using the help of the transliteration, until you are sure you can pronounce them correctly. Memorize the meaning of each word. You may also listen to the pronunciation in the online course of Miami International Seminary. See the PowerPoint presentations in lesson 5 at: http://miamiinternationalseminary.com/course/view.php?id=11.

| | |
|---|---|
| ἅγιος | (*hágios*) "holy" (hagiographs, Hebrew holy writings) |
| αἰών | (*aiṓn*) "age," "eon," "epoch" |
| αἰώνιος | (*aiṓnios*) "eternal" |
| αὐτός, αὐτή, αὐτό | (*autós, autế, autó*) "he," "she," "it," "himself," "herself," "itself" |
| γινώσκω | (*ginṓskō*) "I know" (gnosticism, agnóstic) |
| γυνή | (*gunế*) "woman," "wife" (gynecology) |
| δίδωμι | (*dídōmi*) "I give" |
| δύναμαι | (*dúnamai*) "I can" (dynamite) |
| ἐγώ | (*egṓ*) "I" (egocentric) |

---

[1] A. T. Robertson, *A. Robertson's Word Pictures in Six Volumes* (electronic ed.), *Logos Software*.

| | |
|---|---|
| ἐκεῖνος | (*ekéinos*) "that" |
| ἔρχομαι | (*érchomai*) "I come," "I go" |
| ἐξέρχομαι | (exérchomai) "I leave" |
| ἤ | (*ê*) "or" (Note the accent to distinguish this word from the feminine article ἡ.) |
| κατά | (*katá*) "against," "according to," "during" (*cata*clysm, disaster caused by water flooding *against* something; *cata*logue, a book ordered *according to* theme) |
| λαλέω | (*laléō*) "I speak" |
| μή | (*mê*) "no" |
| μόνον | (*mónon*) "only" |
| νῦν | (*nun*) "now" |
| οὐ | (*u*) "no" |
| πιστεύω | (*pistéuō*) "I believe" |
| σύ | (*su*) "you" |
| οὐρανός | (*uranós*) "heaven" |
| οὗτος, αὕτη, τοῦτο | (*hútos, háutê, túto*) "this" |
| οὕτως | (*hútōs*) "thus" |

## 9.2 Adjectives

Look at Revelation 4:8 in Greek:

Ἅγιος ἅγιος ἅγιος Κύριος ὁ Θεὸς ὁ παντοκράτωρ.
(*hágios, hágios, hágios, kúrios ho theós ho pantocrátōr.*)
Holy, holy, holy, is the Lord God almighty!

Notice that the words for "holy" (ἅγιος) have the same ending (-ος) as "Lord" (Κύριος) and "God" (Θεὸς). This is a grammatical pattern in Greek; the adjectives normally coincide with the nouns they modify in number, gender, and case. If you use software to analyze this word, you will find something like the following. Notice that the information is similar to that provided for a noun.[2]

| Inflected form: | ἅγιος |
|---|---|
| Base form: | ἅγιος |
| Major1: | adjective |
| Case: | nominative |
| Number: | singular |
| Gender: | masculine |

Adjectives modify nouns, describing their characteristics. (The house is *big*.) In English, adjectives do not change with the noun they modify.

---

[2] http://www-users.cs.york.ac.uk/~fisher/cgi-bin/gnt?id=27040826#h.

The book is *big*.
The books are *big*.
The house is *big*.
The houses are *big*.

However, in Greek, the adjective must agree with the noun.

ὁ ἄνθρωπος ἐστὶν ἅγιος.
(*ho ánthrōpos estín hágios.*)
The man is holy.

In this case, the subject "the man" (ὁ ἄνθρωπος) is masculine singular in the nominative case, and therefore the adjective (ἅγιος) is also masculine singular in the nominative case.

In the following example, the subject "the brothers" (οἱ ἀδελφοι) is masculine *plural* nominative, so the adjective (ἅγιοι) must correspond in plural.

οἱ ἀδελφοὶ εἰσὶν ἅγιοι.
(*hoi adelphói eisín hágioi.*)
The brothers are holy.

Now we will modify the phrase so that the adjective (ἁγίου) modifies the possessive noun, "of the man" (τοῦ ἀνθρώπου). The noun "man" is masculine singular in the genitive case, so the adjective must also be masculine singular genitive.

ἐστὶν ὁ ἀδελφὸς τοῦ ἀνθρώπου τοῦ ἁγίου.
(*estín ho adelphós tu anthrṓpu tu hagíu.*)
He is the brother of the holy man.

The adjective can either come between the article and the noun or come after the noun it modifies, with another article in front of it.

ἐστὶν ὁ ἀδελφὸς τοῦ ἁγίου ἀνθρώπου.
(*estín ho adelphós tu hagíu anthrṓpu.*)
He is the brother of the holy man.

ἐστὶν ὁ ἀδελφὸς τοῦ ἀνθρώπου τοῦ ἁγίου.
(*estín ho adelphós tu anthrōpu tu hagíu.*)
He is the brother of the holy man.

In the second case, more emphasis is on the adjective. (He is the brother of the man, that is the man who is holy.)

An adjective can also be used as a noun.

ὁ ἅγιος ἐστὶν ὁ ἀδελφός μου.
(*ho hágios estín ho adelphós mu.*)
The holy one (or holy man) is my brother.

In the diagrams, we will use the symbol \ to indicate a word or phrase that modifies another. The diagram of the clause, "The tall man bought a book," is as follows:

The man | bought |→ a book
\ tall

"Tall" is an adjective that modifies "the man."

See also below the diagram of the following sentence, ὁ ἀδελφὸς βλέπει τόν ἄνθρωπον τὸν ἅγιον (*ho adelphós blépei ton ánthrōpon ton hágion*) "The brother sees the holy man."

ὁ ἀδελφὸς | βλέπει |→ τόν ἄνθρωπον
\ τὸν ἅγιον

ἅγιον modifies ἄνθρωπον.

**9.3 Adverbs**

Adverbs modify verbs. In the following sentence, "quickly" is an adverb, because it tells something about the action of buying the book.

He *quickly* bought the book.

The diagram is as follows:

He | bought |→ the book
\ quickly

In John 3:16, Οὕτως (thus) is an adverb.

Οὕτως γὰρ ἠγάπησεν ὁ Θεὸς τὸν κόσμον
(*Hútōs gar êgápêsen ho theós ton kósmon*)
Thus for loved God the world . . . (literally in this order)

The following are a few common Greek adverbs:

μή (*mê*) "no"
μόνον (*mónon*) "only"
νῦν (*nun*) "now"
οὐ (*u*) "no"
οὕτως (*hútōs*) "thus"

**9.4 Pronouns**

Pronouns replace nouns. ("Man" is a noun, and "he" is a pronoun that may replace it.) In Greek, the pronouns also change according to number and case.

Observe the following tables of personal pronouns. It is not necessary to memorize them, but try to notice some of the clues for recognizing them. Some of the endings are very similar to the article. Notice that −ου indicates genitive singular, −ι indicates dative singular (sometimes it is an iota subscript as in ῳ and ῃ), and −ων indicates genitive plural, for example.

**First Person (I, we)**

**SING.**

| | | Transliteration | Translation |
|---|---|---|---|
| N. | ἐγώ | egō´ | I |
| G. | ἐμοῦ / μου | em<u>u</u> / m<u>u</u> | my |
| D. | ἐμοί / μοι | emói / moi | for me |
| A. | ἐμέ / με | emé / me | me |

**PL.**

| | | | |
|---|---|---|---|
| N. | ἡμεῖς | hêméis | we |
| G. | ἡμῶν | hêmō´n | our |
| D. | ἡμῖν | hêmín | for us |
| A. | ἡμᾶς | hêmás | us |

**Second Person (you)**

**SING.**

| | | Transliteration | Translation |
|---|---|---|---|
| N. | σύ | su | you |
| G. | σοῦ | s<u>u</u> | your |
| D. | σοί | soi | for you |
| A. | σέ | sé | you |

**PL.**

| | | | |
|---|---|---|---|
| N. | ὑμεῖς | huméis | you |
| G. | ὑμῶν | humō´n | your |
| D. | ὑμῖν | humín | for you |
| A. | ὑμᾶς | humás | you |

The third person pronoun also changes according to its gender, as well as case and number.

**Third person (he, she, it, they)**

| SINGULAR | Masculine (he) | Translit./ Translation | Feminine (she) | Translit./ Translation | Neutral (it) | Translit./ Translation |
|---|---|---|---|---|---|---|
| Nominative | αὐτός | autós<br>he | αὐτή | autê´<br>she | αὐτό | autó<br>it |
| Genitive | αὐτοῦ | aut<u>ú</u><br>his | αὐτῆς | autê´s<br>her | αὐτοῦ | aut<u>u</u><br>its |
| Dative | αὐτῷ | autō´<br>for him | αὐτῇ | autê´<br>for her | αὐτῷ | autō´<br>for it |
| Accusative | αὐτόν | autón<br>him | αὐτήν | autê´n<br>her | αὐτό | autó<br>it |
| **PLURAL** | | | | | | |
| Nominative | αὐτοί | autói<br>they | αὐταί | autái<br>they | αὐτά | autá<br>they |
| Genitive | αὐτῶν | autō´n<br>their | αὐτῶν | autō´n<br>their | αὐτῶν | autō´n<br>their |
| Dative | αὐτοῖς | autóis<br>for them | αὐταῖς | autáis<br>for them | αὐτοῖς | autóis<br>for them |
| Accusative | αὐτούς | aut<u>ú</u>s<br>them | αὐτάς | autás<br>them | αὐτά | autá<br>them |

### 9.5 Prepositions

The preposition joins a noun or pronoun to form a phrase that relates to the rest of the sentence. Its very name indicates that it is in a position before the word that it connects. The phrase that contains a preposition can modify a noun or a verb.

He lives *in* a house. ("In a house" modifies the verb "lives.")
He is a man *of* principles. ("Of principles" modifies the noun "man.")

In Greek, each preposition requires a certain grammatical case. That is, the noun after the preposition must appear in the appropriate form, according to the preposition. Some prepositions can use more than one case, and the preposition can have a different meaning with each differing case.

ἐν (*en*, "in" or "on") used with the dative case, indicates location.

ὁ ἄνθρωπος ἐστὶν ἐν τῇ γῇ.
(*ho ánthrōpos estín en tê gê.*)
The man is on (or in) the earth.

ἐκ (*ek*, "from," "of") used with the genitive case, indicates movement away from something.

ὁ κύριος ἐξῆλθον ἐκ τῆς γῆς.
(*ho kúrios exê'lthon ek tês gês.*)
The Lord went from the earth.

εἰς (*eis*, "in," "toward") used with the accusative case, indicates movement toward something.

ὁ κύριος ἔρχει εἰς τὸν οὐρανόν.
(*ho kúrios érchei eis ton uranón.*)
The Lord goes to heaven.

περί (*perí*) means "about" or "concerning" when it is used with the genitive case, and "around" when it is used with the accusative case.

λαλοῦμεν περὶ τοῦ λόγου.
(*lalúmen perí tu lógu.*)
We talk about the word.

ἔρχομαι περὶ τὴν γῆν.
(*érchomai perí tên gên.*)
I go around the earth.

πρός (*pros*) means "toward" when used with the accusative case (as is most common in the New Testament), but it can mean "to the advantage of," or "to be essential to," when used with the genitive case, and "near" or "before" when used with the dative (uses more common in other Greek literature outside the New Testament). This is why Robertson mentions the accusative case in his commentary on John 1:1.

You will have to observe which case is required by each preposition when you learn the vocabulary, or when you look up the word in a dictionary.

Observe the following list and drawing[3] to distinguish the meaning of some important prepositions. Some of these words use several cases and have several different meanings, but for now we will show only the meanings related to movement or location. Memorize the prepositions and their meanings.

περί     (*perí*) "around" (with accusative)

ὑπέρ     (*hupér*) "over" (with accusative)

ἐπί     (*epí*) "on" (with genitive)

πρός     (*pros*) "toward" (with accusative)

εἰς     (*eis*) "into" (with accusative)

ἐν     (*en*) "in" (with dative)

ἐκ     (*ek*) "out of" (with genitive)

ἀπο     (*apó*) "from" (with genitive) (*apó*state, someone who falls away from the truth)

διά     (*diá*) "through" (with genitive) (*dia*meter)

ὑπο     (*hupó*) "under" (with accusative)

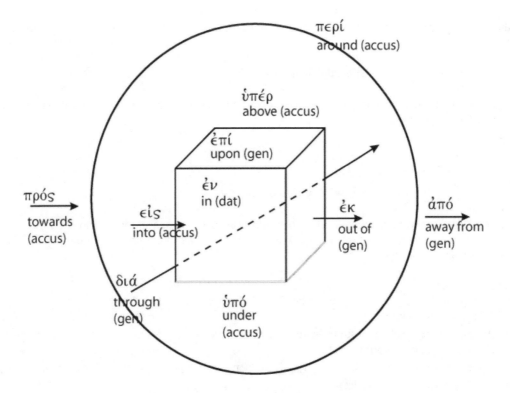

---

[3] The graphic is based on one by Bruce M. Metzger, *Lexical Aids for Students of New Testament Greek* (Princeton, NJ: published by the author, 1969), 80.

**9.6 Adverbial phrases and adjective phrases formed with prepositions**

Prepositions begin phrases that function either as adverbs (modifying verbs, adverbs, or adjectives) or as adjectives (modifying nouns). In the following sentence, the prepositional phrase modifies a verb, and therefore has the same function as an adverb. These phrases frequently explain movement or location.

He walked *in the street.*

> "In" is a preposition.
> "The" is an article.
> "Street" is a noun.
> The phrase explains *where he walked*, and therefore functions like an adverb.

As mentioned previously, we will use the symbol \ to indicate a word or phrase that modifies another. The following diagram illustrates the sentence above:

   He  |  walked

          \ in the street

In the next example, the phrase with a preposition modifies a noun, and therefore functions like an adjective.

The Bible is a book *with much wisdom.*

The phrase "with much wisdom" tells what kind of book the Bible is, and therefore functions like an adjective. The diagram is as follows:

   The Bible  |  is   =  a book

              \ with much wisdom.

**9.7 Using *Logos* software to analyze adjectives, adverbs, pronouns, and prepositions**

The steps for finding the form of Greek adjectives, adverbs, pronouns, and prepositions in *Logos* software are the same as for nouns:

Option 1
1. Start at "Home." Write your verse in the box "Study Passage," and click "Go."
2. Click on "Exegetical guide."
3. Scroll down to the word you want to analyze, such as μονογενῆ. You may need to click on this word in the Greek verse at the top of the window.
4. It gives you the root form and several definitions: "μονογενής: *only begotten.*" (This definition is not the best, as we saw in a previous lesson.)
5. You can look again at dictionary meanings by clicking on any of the dictionaries listed.
6. Listen to the pronunciation.
7. You can also read the explanation of the form. It says "adjective, accusative, singular, masculine."
8. Look also at the other adjectives, adverbs, pronouns, or prepositions in your verse.

Option 2

1. Use the first two steps above.

2. Go to the Bible version in the other window that should be open to the text and change the Bible version to *Nestlé-Aland Greek New Testament, 27ᵗʰ edition with GRAMCORD* or *Nestlé-Aland Greek New Testament 27th edition with McReynolds English Interlinear.* To do this, click on the icon with two rectangles, find the version, and select it.

3. You will see the whole verse you are studying with each word analyzed. For example, the term μονογενῆ has the following analysis:

μονογενῆ
μονογενής
only born
JMSAX (NASM in the McReynolds version)

4. Point to the word you are interested in, right click the mouse, and select "Display information." A message box will open that explains the symbols and gives definitions. "No degree or positive degree" simply means that the form is not comparative ("more") or superlative ("most").

**EXERCISES**

a. Write the definitions below each preposition in the drawing.

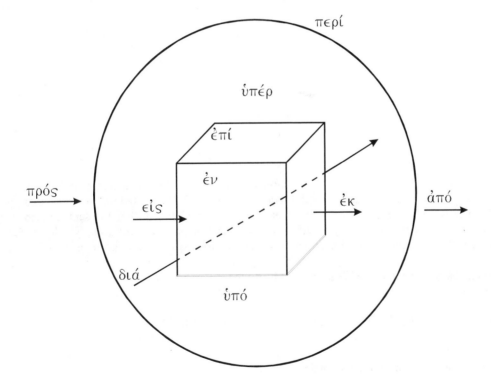

b. Write the definitions:

ἅγιος
αἰών
αἰώνιος
αὐτός, αὐτή, αὐτό
γινώσκω
γυνή
δίδωμι
δύναμαι
ἐγώ
ἐκεῖνος
ἔρχομαι
ἐξέρχομαι
ἤ
κατά
λαλέω
μή
μόνον
νῦν
οὐ
πιστεύω
σύ
οὐρανός
οὗτος, αὕτη, τοῦτο
οὕτως

c. Identify all the adjectives, adverbs, pronouns, and prepositions in the following sentences, both English and Greek. Write "Adj" below the adjectives, "Adv" below the adverbs, "Pron" below pronouns, and "Prep" below the prepositions. Also, translate the Greek sentences into English. For the sentences in Greek, make sure you identify the adjectives, adverbs, pronouns, and prepositions in Greek, which may or may not coincide with the adjectives, adverbs, pronouns, and prepositions in the English translation.

1) The tall man bought a good book in the bookstore that he often visited.

2) She could not read the excellent book, because he did not bring it from the office.

3) He went from the office to the beautiful mountains without her.

4) The good teacher teaches faithfully in the church.

5) She deeply loves the kind man.

6) ὁ ἀνὴρ ὁ ἅγιος λέγει νῦν ἐν τῇ γῇ.

7) ὁ ἀνὴρ τοῦ θεοῦ ἐστιν ἅγιος ἐπὶ τῆς γῆς.

8) ἡ γυνὴ ἡ ἅγια ἔρχεται νῦν εἰς τὸν κύριον ἡμῶν. (ἔρχεται means "comes.")

9) δίδωμι οὕτως αὐτῇ τὸν λόγον τὸν ἅγιον.

10) ἐξέρχομαι ἐκ τῆς γῆς εἰς τὸν οὐρανόν.

d.  Make a sentence diagram of the first clause of John 1:1. ἦν means "was."

Ἐν ἀρχῇ ἦν ὁ λόγος . . .

Remember that _____|_____ represents the nucleus of the sentence with the subject and the verb, that = indicates a predicate nominative, and that \ indicates a word or phrase that modifies another word or phrase. Include the article on the same line with the noun, and not below as an adjective (although technically, the article is a type of adjective).

To help you make the diagram, ask yourself the following questions:
- What is the subject? That is, about whom or what is the sentence talking?
- What is the verb? That is, what is said about the subject?
- What function does the preposition (Ἐν) have? That is, what does the prepositional phrase modify?

Be careful on this last part. Ask yourself, does the prepositional phrase indicate something about the subject, or about the verb? If it modifies the subject, it will say what kind of person he or she is. If it modifies the verb, it will possibly say when it happened or how it happened. If the phrase modifies the subject, connect the curved line with the subject. If it modifies the verb, connect it with the verb.

e. Identify any adjective, adverb, pronoun, or preposition in your Greek study text. Use the verse you have already written in Greek, and write "Adj" below the adjectives, "Adv" below the adverbs, "Pron" below pronouns, and "Prep" below the prepositions. You might need the help of a Greek dictionary, *The New Linguistic and Exegetical Key*, an analytical lexicon, or linguistic software.

# LESSON 10

# MORPHOLOGY (PART 3): VERBS AND TENSES

*In this lesson, you will learn the principal forms of the Greek verb. When you finish, you will identify the tense, person, number, and meaning of a list of Greek verbs.*

The verbs are the principal part of a sentence. They are like the steel beams that hold up the weight of a building. Without the verb, the sentence falls to the ground, because it has no meaning. The study of just one verb can change our interpretation of a text, or it might even affect our theology. For example, 1 John 3:6 says,

> *No one who abides in Him sins; no one who sins has seen Him or knows Him. (NASB)*

Does this mean that a Christian never sins? The key to interpreting this verse is in the form of the verb.

First, you need to learn some new vocabulary.

## 10.1 Vocabulary

Learn this list of words. Learn to pronounce them, and memorize their meanings. You may also listen to the pronunciation in the online course of Miami International Seminary. See the PowerPoint presentations in lesson 6 at: http://miamiinternationalseminary.com/course/view.php?id=11.

| | |
|---|---|
| ἀποστέλλω | (*apostélō*) "I send" (an apostle is a "sent one") |
| θέλω | (*thélō*) "I desire" |
| καλέω | (*kaléō*) "I call," "I invite" |
| λαμβάνω | (*lambánō*) "I take," "I receive" |
| λύω | (*lúō*) "I loose," "I free" |
| μετά | (*metá*) "with" (when used with genitive), "after" (when used with accusative) |
| | (The philosophical term "metaphysics" has its origin in the fact that in Aristotle's writings, the study of being came *after* the study of *physics*.) |
| οὖν | (*un*) "then" |
| πατήρ | (*patêr*) "father" (*pa*ternal) |
| πίστις | (*pístis*) "faith," "belief" |
| πνεῦμα | (*néuma*) "spirit" |
| | Note: Remember that the combination of letters πν is pronounced like an "n." |

79

| | |
|---|---|
| πολύς | (*polús*) "much," "many" (*poly*theism, *poly*gamy) |
| σῶμα | (*sō'ma*) "body" (psycho*soma*tic, sickness of the body related to psychological factors) |
| φωνή | (*phōnê'*) "voice" (phonics) |

## 10.2 The verb

The verb describes the action or the condition of the subject. As well as being the most important and most interesting part of the sentence, it is also the most complex aspect. The Greek verb has tenses, voices, and moods, as well as indicating person and number.

The analysis of the verb reveals the meaning of a sentence. For example, in John 5:24, Jesus says that those who believe in Him *have passed* from death to life. What are the implications of this verb form? It is in the *perfect* tense, which indicates an action in the past that continues to have consequences now. The statement of Jesus suggests the image of a line that people cross over when they believe. They were on the side of death, and now they are on the side of life.

Death     Life

## 10.3 Tenses

In English, there are the following verb tenses:

| TENSE | EXAMPLE |
|---|---|
| Simple | |
|   Present | I look |
|   Past | I looked |
|   Future | I will look |
| Progressive | |
|   Present progressive | I am looking |
|   Past progressive | I was looking |
|   Future progressive | I shall (or will) be looking |
| Perfect | |
|   Present perfect | I have looked |
|   Past perfect | I had looked |
|   Future perfect | I shall (or will) have looked |

Notice that a verb tense includes two elements: aspect and time. The aspect can be simple, progressive, or perfect. Simple is like a snapshot, progressive is ongoing like a movie, and perfect is a completed action, like a book that has been closed.

In Greek, there are similar tenses, but some of the names are changed. Instead of "past progressive," Greek has "imperfect." Instead of "past perfect," Greek has "pluperfect." Instead of "past," Greek has "aorist." Greek does have a future perfect, but it is only used a few times in the New Testament, so it will not be studied in this text. Furthermore, it is composed of a phrase (called "paraphrastic future perfect"), rather than being indicated by modifications within just one word like the other tenses in Greek. The Greek present tense is used for both concepts of simple present and present progressive.

The Greek *aorist* is not exactly the same as the English *past*. In some moods, it may not necessarily indicate much about time, or action in the past. It definitely does not indicate past progressive, because the imperfect fulfills that function. Some have described the aorist as being punctiliar. However, probably the best way to summarize its meaning is to say it describes an action *in its totality*. This will be discussed more completely in the next lesson.

At the risk of over-simplifying, we will show the parallel Greek terms for the verb tenses.

| ENGLISH TENSE | EXAMPLE | GREEK TENSE |
|---|---|---|
| Simple | | |
| Present | I look | Present |
| Past | I looked | Aorist |
| Future | I will look | Future |
| Progressive | | |
| Present progressive | I am looking | (Present) |
| Past progressive | I was looking | Imperfect |
| Future progressive | I shall (or will) be looking | |
| Perfect | | |
| Present perfect | I have looked | Perfect |
| Past perfect | I had looked | Pluperfect |
| Future perfect | I shall (or will) have looked | * |

*Future perfect will not be studied in this course, since it occurs infrequently in the New Testament.

We could symbolize the meaning of the Greek tenses the following way. Notice that we will begin to change the order of the tenses as we list them, since Greek grammars usually follow this pattern:

**Present**

Either "I look," or            A            simple action in the present, or

"I am looking"            - - - - - - - -            progressive action at present time

**Imperfect**

"I was looking"            - - - - - - - )            continuous action in the past

**Future**

"I will look"            ———> A            future action

**Aorist**

"I looked"            [ A ]            action seen in its totality
                                       (sometimes, not always, in the past)

**Perfect**

"I have looked"            A ———>            action (A) *completed* in the past,
                                              whose effects continue now

**Pluperfect**

"I had looked"            A1 —— A2 )            past action (A1) previous to another
                                                 past action (A2)

You may remember from English grammar that verbs have person and number. First person is "I" or "we," second person is "you" singular or plural, and third person is "he, she, it, or they." Look at the different forms of the verb "loose" in English in the present tense.

1 sing        I loose

2 sing        you loose

3 sing        he, she, or it looses

| | | |
|---|---|---|
| 1 plural | we loose | |
| 2 plural | you (pl) loose | |
| 3 plural | they loose | |

The verb for "loose" in Greek is λύω. The following table gives the present tense. **Memorize these forms.**

| | | |
|---|---|---|
| 1 sing | λύω | I loose |
| 2 sing | λύεις | you loose |
| 3 sing | λύει | he, she, or it looses |
| 1 plural | λύομεν | we loose |
| 2 plural | λύετε | you (pl) loose |
| 3 plural | λύουσι(ν) | they loose |

Now we'll show you the full table of the forms of the verb λύω (*lúō*, "I free," or "I loose") with all the verb tenses in indicative mood. (We will study the meaning of the moods later.) This paradigm is called the *conjugation* of the verb.

Notice that some verbs have a second form with a (ν) in parentheses. This is sometimes used when the following word begins with a vowel, or when the verb comes at the end of a sentence. For example, we may find λύουσιν ἐκ. . . . We assume this change was to make the pronunciation easier.

Observe the forms. It is not necessary to memorize all of them, but you should at least learn the forms of the present tense. This table only gives the forms for indicative mood. We will study other moods in another lesson.

**Paradigm of the regular verb, λύω (indicative mood)**

| | Present | Imperfect | Future | Aorist | Perfect | Pluperfect |
|---|---|---|---|---|---|---|
| 1 s | λύω<br><br>*lúō*<br>I loose | ἔλυον<br><br>*éluon*<br>I was loosing | λύσω<br><br>*lúsō*<br>I shall loose | ἔλυσα<br><br>*élusa*<br>I loosed | λέλυκα<br><br>*léluka*<br>I have loosed | ἐλελύκειν<br><br>*elelúkein*<br>I had loosed |
| 2 s | λύεις<br><br>*lúeis*<br>you loose | ἔλυες<br><br>*élues*<br>you were loosing | λύσεις<br><br>*lúseis*<br>you shall loose | ἔλυσας<br><br>*élusas*<br>you loosed | λέλυκας<br><br>*lélukas*<br>you have loosed | ἐλελύκεις<br><br>*elelúkeis*<br>you had loosed |
| 3 s | λύει<br><br>*lúei*<br>he looses | ἔλυε(ν)<br><br>*élue(n)*<br>he was loosing | λύσει<br><br>*lúsei*<br>he shall loose | ἔλυσε(ν)<br><br>*éluse(n)*<br>he loosed | λέλυκε(ν)<br><br>*léluke(n)*<br>he has loosed | ἐλελύκει<br><br>*elelúkei*<br>he had loosed |

| | | | | | | |
|---|---|---|---|---|---|---|
| 1 pl | λύομεν<br><br>*lúomen*<br>we loose | ἐλύομεν<br><br>*elúomen*<br>we were loosing | λύσομεν<br><br>*lúsomen*<br>we shall loose | ἐλύσαμεν<br><br>*elúsamen*<br>we loosed | λελύκαμεν<br><br>*lelúkamen*<br>we have loosed | ἐλελύκειμεν<br><br>*elelúkeimen*<br>we had loosed |
| 2 pl | λύετε<br><br>*lúete*<br>you loose | ἐλύετε<br><br>*elúete*<br>you were loosing | λύσετε<br><br>*lúsete*<br>you shall loose | ἐλύσατε<br><br>*elúsate*<br>you loosed | λελύκατε<br><br>*lelúkate*<br>you have loosed | ἐλελύκειτε<br><br>*elelúkeite*<br>you had loosed |
| 3 pl | λύουσι(ν)<br><br>*lúusi(n)*<br>they loose | ἔλυον<br><br>*éluon*<br>they were loosing | λύσουσι(ν)<br><br>*lúsusi(n)*<br>they shall loose | ἔλυσαν<br><br>*élusan*<br>they loosed | λελύκασι(ν)<br><br>*lelúkasi(n)*<br>they have loosed | ἐλελύκεισαν<br><br>*elelúkeisan*<br>they had loosed |

If you pay attention to the final letters, you can have a good idea of the person and the number of the verb. The following list shows frequent endings of the regular verb.[1]

| | |
|---|---|
| 1 s. | –ω, –α, –ον |
| 2 s. | –ς |
| 3 s. | –ει, –ε, –εν |
| 1 pl. | –μεν |
| 2 pl. | –τε |
| 3 pl. | –σι(ν), –σαν, –ον |

There are other changes that normally indicate the tense of the verb. If you study the conjugation of λύω you will see the following patterns:

a. An augment (addition) to the prefix, when there are no other changes, indicates imperfect tense (ἔλυον, "I was loosing"). The "augment" means adding –ε– before a word, or changing the vowel so that it becomes long (for example, a verb that begins with an –ε– will change the –ε– to an –η–.

b. When a –σ– is added at the end of the verb root, without an augment in the prefix, it indicates future tense (λύσω, "I will loose").

c. When a –σ– is added to the root, *plus* an augment in the prefix, it indicates aorist tense (ἔλυσα, "I loosed").

d. A reduplication at the beginning of a word, plus a –κ– added to the root, indicates perfect tense (λέλυκα, "I have loosed"). A reduplication is a repetition of the sound of the first letters, or some

---

[1] Many Greek grammar books (such as William D. Mounce, *Basics of Biblical Greek* (Grand Rapids: Zondervan, 1993), see 126–28) make a distinction between the "variable vowel" and the "ending." They also make a distinction between "primary" endings and "secondary" endings. However, for our introductory purposes, we simply encourage the student to look for the endings shown above to identify the person and number.

addition to produce a similar sound. Sometimes the first letter is repeated along with an −ε−. For example, with the verb λύω the reduplication is λε−, and with the verb πιστεύω the reduplication is πε−.

e. An augment, plus a reduplication, plus a κ added to the regular root indicates pluperfect (ἐλελύκειν, "I had loosed"). The pluperfect does not always have an augment, but when it doesn't, it can be identified by the endings that have −ει (−ειν, −εις, −ει, −ειμεν, −ειτε, −εισαν).

The following table summarizes the guidelines for recognizing the tenses in indicative mood:

| | Pres | Imp | Fut | Aor | Perf | Plup |
|---|---|---|---|---|---|---|
| Augment | | ε | | ε | | ε |
| Reduplication | | | | | R | R |
| Addition to the root | | | σ | σ | κ | κ |

The root of the verb λύω is λυ−. If we use "V" to symbolize the root of the verb and "R" to represent a reduplication, we can symbolize the verb forms as follows:

| | | | | |
|---|---|---|---|---|
| V | = present | λύω | I loose |
| ε V | = imperfect | ἔλυον | I was loosing |
| V σ | = future | λύσω | I shall loose |
| ε V σ | = aorist | ἔλυσα | I loosed |
| R V κ | = perfect | λέλυκα | I have loosed |
| ε R V κ | = pluperfect | ἐλελύκειν | I had loosed |

Instead of trying to memorize all the verb forms, you should memorize how to recognize them.

## 10.4 Irregular verbs

English has many irregular verbs. The *regular* way to form a past tense is to add "ed" to the end of the present tense. For example, "jump" becomes "jumped." However, the irregular verbs do not follow this pattern. For instance, "run" becomes "ran," "swim" becomes "swam," and "win" becomes "won."

Greek also has many verbs that do not follow the regular pattern. For example, many verbs have an aorist form with the root modified. This is called the "second aorist."

| | | | |
|---|---|---|---|
| ἔρχομαι (*érchomai*) | becomes | ἦλθον (*ê'lthon*) | in aorist |
| βάλλω (*bálō*) | becomes | ἔβαλον (*ébalon*) | in aorist |

If we were to use the guideline of the regular verb to analyze these aorist forms, we would be confused, because they do not have the −σ− added to the verb stem. The endings are not the same as the regular verb either, especially in the first person singular and third person plural. (See the conjugation in the following section.) The only thing that helps us identify these verbs is the augment on the front of the word that is typical of the aorist.

Other irregular verbs make modifications in their future tense. For example,

ἀποστέλλω (*apostélō*) becomes ἀποστελῶ (*apostelō´*)

It would be awkward to add an −σ− to the stem of this verb.

There are so many irregular forms that it is virtually impossible to memorize them. The important thing for now is to *know that they exist*. When you look up the root form of a verb, you might be surprised at how different it is from the word you are analyzing. You might think you have made a mistake, unless you take into account the fact that it may be an irregular verb.

**10.5 Using *Logos* software to analyze verbs**
The steps for finding the form of a Greek verb in *Logos* software are the same as for nouns and other words we have already studied:

Option 1
1. Start at "Home."
2. Write in your reference in "Study Passage" and click "Go."
3. Under "Other Tools" click on "Exegetical Guide."
4. Find the word you want to analyze, such as ἠγάπησεν.
5. It gives you the root form and several definitions: "ἀγαπάω: *to love*."
6. Listen to the pronunciation.
7. Read the analysis of the form. It says "verb, aorist, active, indicative, third person, singular."
8. You might want to look again at any of the dictionaries listed to remind yourself of different possible definitions.
9. Look also at the other verbs in your verse.

Option 2
1. Go to the Greek version *Nestlé-Aland Greek New Testament, 27ᵗʰ edition with GRAMCORD* or *Nestlé-Aland Greek New Testament, 27th Edition with McReynolds English Interlinear*. To do this, click on the icon with two rectangles, find the *Nestlé-Aland* version, and select it.
2. You will see the whole verse you are studying with each word analyzed. For example, the term "loved" appears as the following:

ἠγάπησεν
ἀγαπάω
loved
V3SAAI  (VAA13S in McReynolds version)

3. Point to the verb in the text, right click on the mouse, and select "Display information." An information box will open that gives a complete analysis of the word.

Remember to use the *Logos* tutorials to learn how to use their program.

## EXERCISES

a. Complete the following table with the most frequent endings that indicate person and number of the verbs.

|  | **Possible Endings** |
|---|---|
| 1 sing |  |
| 2 sing |  |
| 3 sing |  |
| 1 plural |  |
| 2 plural |  |
| 3 plural |  |

b. Describe the meaning of each verb tense in Greek:

present

imperfect

future

aorist

perfect

pluperfect

c. Write the forms of the present indicative of λύω.

| 1 sing |  |
|---|---|
| 2 sing |  |
| 3 sing |  |
| 1 plural |  |
| 2 plural |  |
| 3 plural |  |

d. Write the guidelines for recognizing the tense of the verbs in indicative mood.

|  | Pres | Imp | Fut | Aor | Perf | Plup |
|---|---|---|---|---|---|---|
| Augment |  |  |  |  |  |  |
| Reduplication |  |  |  |  |  |  |
| Addition to the root |  |  |  |  |  |  |

e. Considering "V" as the symbol of the root of the verb, and "R" as the symbol of a reduplication, indicate the forms of the regular verb:

present =
imperfect =
future =
aorist =
perfect =
pluperfect =

f. Write the meanings of the following vocabulary words:

ἀποστέλλω
θέλω
καλέω
λαμβάνω
λύω
μετά
οὖν
πατήρ
πίστις
πνεῦμα
πολύς
σῶμα
φωνή

g. Indicate the tense, person, and number of the following verbs, and translate them. If you have problems, review the lesson.

|  | Tense | Person | Number | Translation |
|---|---|---|---|---|
| λύω |  |  |  |  |
| λύει |  |  |  |  |
| λύομεν |  |  |  |  |
| λύουσι |  |  |  |  |
| ἐλύομεν |  |  |  |  |
| ἐλύετε |  |  |  |  |
| λύσει |  |  |  |  |
| λύσουσιν |  |  |  |  |
| ἔλυσας |  |  |  |  |
| ἐλύσαμεν |  |  |  |  |

h. Make a diagram of the following phrase in John 1:1.

ὁ λόγος ἦν πρὸς τὸν θεόν,
(*ho lógos ên pros ton* <u>*theón*</u>)

If you do not know the meaning of a word, you can look it up in a dictionary.

Remember that _____|_____ represents the subject and the verb,

that = _____ represents a predicate nominative, and that \ represents the modification of a word or phrase.

i. Identify the verbs in your study verse, and discover their person, tense, and number. Use *The New Linguistic and Exegetical Key*, Bible software, or an analytical lexicon. Write the information below the verb in the Greek verse you have written out.

# LESSON 11

# MORPHOLOGY (PART 4): MORE ABOUT VERBS

*In this lesson you will continue learning more about verbs, the major building materials of the sentence. You will learn about moods, voices, and deponent verbs. When you finish the lesson, you will explain the meaning of the different moods and voices in Greek. You will also identify the forms of some Greek verbs and translate them into English.*

**11.1 Vocabulary**

Memorize this list of new words. Practice pronouncing them. You may also listen to the pronunciation in the online course of Miami International Seminary. See the PowerPoint presentations in lesson 7 at: http://miamiinternationalseminary.com/course/view.php?id=11.

| | |
|---|---|
| ἄγγελος | (*ángelos*) "messenger," "angel" |
| ἁμαρτία | (*hamartía*) "sin" |
| βασιλεία | (*basileía*) "kingdom" (basilica, originally a king's palace) |
| γίνομαι | (*gínomai*) "I become" |
| γράφω | (*gráphō*) "I write" (*graph*ics, cali*graph*y) |
| δόξα | (*dóxa*) "glory" (*dox*ology) |
| ἔθνος | (*éthnos*) "nation," "ethnic group," "gentile" |
| ἔργον | (*érgon*) "work" (synergy) |
| ἐσθίω | (*esthíō*) "I eat" |
| εὑρίσκω | (*heurískō*) "find" (eureka!) |
| ἵστημι | (*hístêmi*) "I stand" |
| καθώς | (*kathṓs*) "as," "just as" |
| καρδία | (*kardía*) "heart" (cardiology, cardiac) |

**11.2 Verb voices**

In English, verbs can be either in *active voice* or *passive voice*. Active voice is used when the subject acts. The passive voice is used when the subject receives the action passively. For example, in the sentence using active voice, "The man bought a book," "the man" is the subject, "bought" is the verb in active voice, and "book" is the direct object.

The man | bought |→ a book

89

But we can express the same idea using passive voice: "The book was bought by the man."

<u>The book</u> | <u>was bought</u>
      \ by the man

In this case, "the book" is the subject that receives the action of the verb "was bought."

In Greek, verbs can also be in active or passive voice, but there is also a third voice called middle voice. The middle voice expresses the idea that the subject is indirectly affected by the action or that the subject acted upon himself or herself. It is translated to English with expressions such as "for himself" or "for herself." ("The man bought a book for himself.") Interestingly, in Greek, these concepts of active, passive, and middle voice are expressed completely within one word.

For example:

| | |
|---|---|
| ἔλυσα | (*élusa*) means "I loosed" (active voice), |
| ἐλύθην | (*elúthên*) means "I was loosed" (passive voice), and |
| ἐλυσάμην | (*elusámên*) means "I loosed myself" or "I loosed something for myself" (middle voice). |

In most tenses (all but aorist and future) the form of the middle voice and the form of the passive voice are the same. Only the context will indicate which one it is. For example, λύομαι (*lúomai*) can be taken as passive voice ("I am loosed") or as middle voice ("I loose for myself"). The following table compares the present active and the present middle/passive forms of λύω.

| **Pres Act** | | **Pres M/P** | |
|---|---|---|---|
| λύω | (*lúō*) I loose | λύομαι | (*lúomai*) I loose myself/ I am loosed |
| λύεις | (*lúeis*) you loose | λύῃ | (*lúê*) you loose yourself/ you are loosed |
| λύει | (*lúei*) he, she looses | λύεται | (*lúetai*) he, she looses himself, herself/ he, she is loosed |
| λύομεν | (*lúomen*) we loose | λυόμεθα | (*luómetha*) we loose ourselves/ we are loosed |
| λύετε | (*lúete*) you loose | λύεσθε | (*lúesthe*) you loose yourselves/ you are loosed |
| λύουσι(ν) | (*lúusi -n*) they loose | λύονται | (*lúontai*) they loose themselves/ they are loosed |

Notice the frequent use of –αι and –θ in the middle/passive forms.

90

**11.3 Deponent verbs**

Some verbs use the *form* of middle or passive voice with the *meaning* of active voice. These are a kind of irregularity, and they are called "deponent" verbs. You must be careful in translating these verbs, because you might think they have the meaning of middle or passive voice (the subject acting upon himself or being acted upon), but they should be translated simply as active voice.

For example:

ἔρχομαι (*érchomai*, "I come") is a deponent verb in present tense and in future tense (ἐλεύσομαι, *eléusomai*, "I shall come"). It has the form of middle voice, but the meaning of active voice.

γίνομαι (*gínomai*, "I become") is also deponent in present and future (γενήσομαι, *genê'somai*, "I shall become").

εἰμί (*eimí*, "I am") is defective in the future tense (ἔσομαι, *ésomai*, "I shall be").

How can you know if a verb is deponent? Only by looking up the word in a dictionary, where the principal parts are shown. For example, in the dictionary, the verb "to be" (εἰμί) is shown with the future as ἔσομαι. From the ending –μαι, you know that it is deponent in future.

**11.4 Verb moods**

In addition to tense, person, number, and voice, verbs are also classified by *mood*. In Greek, there are the following moods: indicative, subjunctive, imperative, infinitive, and participle.

| Mood | Meaning | Greek | English |
|------|---------|-------|---------|
| Indicative | Indicates something | λύει | He or she looses. |
| Subjunctive | Shows probability, purpose, emotion, contrary to reality | λύῃ | (Possibly...) he or she might loose/ (so that...) he or she looses or will loose/ (as if...) he or she loosed. |
| Imperative | Command | λῦε | Loose! |
|  |  | λυέτω | May he or she loose! |
| Infinitive | Unlimited (used grammatically as a noun) | λύειν | To loose |
| Participle | Similar to a participle in English (used grammatically as an adjective) | λύων | Loosing |

Note that in Greek, the imperative may also be in third person, λυέτω (*luétō*), "May he loose."

The following sentences show the difference in the moods.

Indicative ὁ ἄνθρωπος **λύει** τὸν δοῦλον.
(*ho ánthrōpos lúei ton dúlon.*)
The man **frees** the slave.

Subjunctive ἔρχομαι ἵνα ὁ ἄνθρωπος **λύῃ** τὸν δοῦλον.
(*érchomai hína ho ánthrōpos lúê ton dúlon.*)
I come so that the man **might free** the slave.

Imperative ὁ ἄνθρωπος **λυέτω** τὸν δοῦλον.
(*ho ánthrōpos luétō ton dúlon.*)
**May** the man **free** the slave!

Infinitive θέλω **λύειν** τὸν δοῦλον.
(*thélō lúein ton dúlon.*)
I desire **to free** the slave.

Participle **λύων** τὸν δοῦλον, ὁ ἄνθρωπος βλέπει τὸν ἀδελφὸν σου.
(*lúōn ton dúlon, ho ánthrōpos blépei ton adelphón su.*)
**Freeing** the slave, the man sees his brother.

## 11.5 How to identify the mood

It is not always easy to identify the mood of a Greek verb. Therefore, it is important to learn to use the linguistic tools such as *The New Linguistic and Exegetical Key* or linguistic software such as *Logos* or *BibleWorks*. Nevertheless, there are some guidelines that can help us:

1. The subjunctive normally turns the first vowel of the ending into a long vowel, typically η or ω.
   For example, λύομεν ("we free") changes to λύωμεν ("we might free").
2. The imperative normally adds –ετ. For example, λύει ("he frees") changes to λυέτω ("May he or she free!").
3. The infinitive normally ends in –ειν or –αι.
4. The participle normally adds –ων, –ου, or –ον before the ending. The participle will be studied more in a future lesson.

Observe the forms of the different moods of λύω in present tense, active voice:

| | | |
|---|---|---|
| Indicative | 1 sing | λύω<br>I free |
| | 2 sing | λύεις<br>you free |
| | 3 sing | λύει<br>he, she frees |
| | 1 plural | λύομεν<br>we free |
| | 2 plural | λύετε<br>you free |
| | 3 plural | λύουσι(ν)<br>they free |

| | | |
|---|---|---|
| Subjunctive | 1 sing | λύω<br>I might free |
| | 2 sing | λύῃς<br>you might free |
| | 3 sing | λύῃ<br>he, she might free |
| | 1 plural | λύωμεν<br>we might free |
| | 2 plural | λύητε<br>you might free |
| | 3 plural | λύωσι(ν)<br>they might free |

| | | |
|---|---|---|
| Imperative | 2 sing | λῦε<br>Free! |
| | 3 sing | λυέτω<br>May he, she free! |
| | 2 plural | λύετε<br>Free! |
| | 3 plural | λυέτωσαν<br>May they free! |

| | |
|---|---|
| Inf. | λύειν<br>to free |

## 11.6 The complete conjugation of λύω

In the appendix, you can look at a table with all of the forms (called the "paradigm" or "conjugation") of the regular verb λύω with the corresponding translations. Remember that the translation always depends on the context, and sometimes the form may be ambiguous. Don't worry about memorizing these forms. In this text, it is sufficient to know some guidelines about recognizing the forms and interpreting their meanings. You can use the appropriate linguistic tools that have been introduced in these lessons to identify the verb forms of your text.

## 11.7 The meaning of the aorist tense

Now that we have studied the verb moods, we need to explain a little more about the meaning of the aorist tense. The temptation is to consider it the equivalent of past tense in English. However, even though the aorist frequently does refer to past tense, especially in the indicative mood, in other moods the Greek aorist does not put the emphasis on the time or duration of the action. In general, the aorist expresses an action simply as something that happens.

Some linguists have suggested that the aorist tense points to "punctiliar" action. However, this is not the normally accepted explanation now. Linguists prefer to emphasize the general limitless meaning. "Aorist" literally means "without boundary." Richard Young explains that the difference between the present tense and the aorist tense in Greek is like the difference between observing a parade from the side of the street and observing the same parade from a helicopter. The present tense watches each participant individually pass by, while the aorist watches the event in its totality.[1]

Experts suggest that the aorist is the most important of Greek tenses and that it is the "most characteristic of the Greek tenses." Dana and Mantey explain that "the fundamental meaning of the aorist is to denote action simply as occurring, without reference to its progress. . . . It has no special temporal significance, finding its time relationships only in the Indicative where it is used as past tense."[2] They say that the aorist "establishes the fact of the action or event, without consideration of its duration," and that it "denotes an action simply as an event, without defining in any way the manner of its occurrence."[3]

The difference between λυέτω (*luétō*, present imperative, third person singular, active voice) and λυσάτω (*lusátō*, aorist imperative, third person singular, active voice) is that the present suggests progression, while the aorist suggests something more indefinite. Since it is difficult to communicate the difference in English, the translations may be the same, or they might be different. The context will determine the meaning.

λυέτω  "May he or she free . . . !"
       "May he or she continue freeing . . . !"

λυσάτω  "May he or she free!"
        "May he or she begin to free!"

This difference becomes important when we compare verses such as 1 John 2:1; 3:6; and 3:9.

2:1 τεκνία μου, ταῦτα γράφω ὑμῖν ἵνα μὴ ἁμάρτητε.
    καὶ ἐάν τις ἁμάρτῃ, παράκλητον ἔχομεν πρὸς τὸν πατέρα. . . .

    (*teknía mu, tauta gráphō humín hína mê hamártête.*
    *kai eán tis hamártê, paráklêton échomen pros ton patéra . . .* )

    My little children, these things write I unto you, that ye sin not.
    And if any man sin, we have an advocate with the Father, Jesus Christ the righteous: (KJV)

3:6 πᾶς ὁ ἐν αὐτῷ μένων οὐχ ἁμαρτάνει·
    πᾶς ὁ ἁμαρτάνων οὐχ ἑώρακεν αὐτὸν οὐδὲ ἔγνωκεν αὐτόν.

    (*pas ho en autṓ ménōn uch hamartánei*
    *pas ho hamartánōn uch heṓraken autón ude égnōken autón.*)

    Whosoever abideth in him sinneth not;
    whosoever sinneth hath not seen him, neither known him. (KJV)

---

[1] Richard Young, *Intermediate New Testament Greek* (Nashville: Broadman and Holman, 1994), 122.
[2] Dana and Mantey, *Gramática griega del Nuevo Testamento* (El Paso: Casa Bautista, 1975), 186.
[3] Ibid., 187.

3:9 πᾶς ὁ γεγεννημένος ἐκ τοῦ θεοῦ ἁμαρτίαν οὐ ποιεῖ . . .

(*pas ho gegenêménos ek tu̲ theú̲ harmartían u̲ poiéi . . .*)

Whosoever is born of God doth not commit sin; for his seed remaineth in him: and he cannot sin, because he is born of God. (KJV)

At first sight, this might look like a contradiction, especially in a translation like the King James Version. In chapter 2, John seems to assume that Christians will continue to sin, but in chapter 3, he appears to be saying that a Christian does not sin any longer. Someone might conclude that if he sins, he is not a Christian.

The most probable solution to this problem is found in the verbs and their tenses. In 1 John 2:1, the verbs translated "that ye sin not" and "if any man sin" are in the aorist tense (ἁμάρτητε, ἁμάρτῃ), but in 3:6, both verbs translated "sinneth" in the King James Version (ἁμαρτάνει, ἁμαρτάνων) are in the present tense (indicative and participle, respectively). We interpret the different tenses to mean that in 2:1 John supposes that Christians will sin *occasionally*, but in 3:6 he is saying that the Christian does not *practice* sin *as his lifestyle*. The Lord has given him victory over sin, and he is no longer a *slave* to it. (See Romans 6:14: "For sin shall not be master over you, for you are not under law, but under grace," NASB) The New International Version translates 1 John 3:6 as, "No one who lives in him *keeps on sinning*. No one who *continues to sin* has either seen him or known him."

As for 1 John 3:9, a different phrase is used in Greek, ἁμαρτίαν οὐ ποιεῖ, which literally says, "does not do sin." Again, the verb for "do" or "make" (ποιεῖ) is in the present tense, suggesting an ongoing lifestyle of sin. The New International Version translates 3:9 as "No one who is born of God will *continue to sin*. . . ." The New American Standard Bible reads, "No one who is born of God *practices sin*. . . ."

Notice also the two participles in 3:6, μένων and ἁμαρτάνων. We could translate literally, "Everyone who *is remaining* in Christ does not continue sinning. Everyone who *is sinning* has not seen Him or known Him." The idea is that while someone is *remaining in Christ*, he is not sinning. That is, in the moment he is trusting in Christ and depending on Him, he is not subject to the dominating power of sin (see also John 15). However, according to other passages (such as 1 John 2:1; 1 John 1:9; and Romans 7), we know that even a Christian gives in to temptation and sins. The point is that, in the moment in which he gives in to temptation, he is not remaining in Christ and depending on Him. In a sense, when a Christian gives in to sin, he is acting as if he were not a Christian; he is not living according to his new identity in Christ. This does not mean he is no longer a Christian, but that in the act of sinning, he is out of character with his new life in Christ.

The analysis of the Greek verbs helps us find probable solutions to the apparent contradiction. Our findings allow us to harmonize these passages with other clear teachings of the New Testament, namely that a Christian does in fact sin sometimes.

### 11.8 Morphology of the verbs in John 3:16

Now we can understand the verb ἠγάπησεν found in John 3:16. *The New Linguistic and Exegetical Key* reads:

ἠγάπησεν aor. ind. act. ἀγαπάω (#26) to love

The online *Greek New Testament* gives the following information: [4]

---

[4] http://www-users.cs.york.ac.uk/~fisher/gnt/chapters.html.

| | |
|---|---|
| Inflected form: | ἠγάπησεν |
| Base form: | ἀγαπάω |
| Major1: | verb |
| Person: | 3rd |
| Tense: | aorist |
| Voice: | active |
| Mood: | indicative |
| Number: | singular |

The *BibleWorks NT Morphology* version of the New Testament shows the following:

ἠγάπησεν
ἀγαπάω
viaa3s

*Logos* software (The *Nestlé-Aland* version with GRAMCORD) shows something similar:

ἠγάπησεν
ἀγαπάω
loved
V3SAAI

We can see from any of these sources that the verb is in aorist tense, indicative mood, active voice, and that it comes from ἀγαπάω, which means "to love." We can translate the verb as "loved," and we now comprehend that it refers to the action as a totality, not necessarily as a punctiliar action or as a finished action.

We can use these same tools to find that the verb "gave" in John 3:16 (ἔδωκεν) is also aorist indicative, active voice. "Perish" (ἀπόληται) is an aorist subjunctive, in middle voice, from ἀπόλλυμι, and "have" (ἔχη) is a present subjunctive, active voice, from ἔχω. Both of these latter two verbs are subjunctive because they belong to a purpose clause that begins with ἵνα ("in order that"). The present tense of "have" suggests an ongoing eternal life. πιστεύων is a present active participle, masculine nominative. Therefore, "whoever believes" (πᾶς ὁ πιστεύων) is literally "every one who is believing." Again the present tense suggests a continuous faith instead of a temporary faith.

A somewhat paraphrased translation of our verse would be:

*Thus God loved the world so much that He gave His only Son, so that everyone who is believing in Him should not be destroyed, but continually have eternal life.*

**11.9 Conjunctions**

Conjunctions are words that unite, such as "and," "or," "therefore." We will study in the next lesson how these words are used to make complex sentences. Often these little words are the key to understanding a Bible passage and its relation to the nearby context.

The Greek conjunctions that we have learned so far are:

| | |
|---|---|
| γάρ | "for," "since," "then" |
| δέ | "and," "but" |
| ἵνα | "so that," "that" |
| καί | "and" |
| οὖν | "therefore" |
| οὕτως | "thus" |

**EXERCISES**

a. Write the definitions:

ἄγγελος
ἁμαρτία
βασιλεία
γίνομαι
γράφω
δόξα
ἔθνος
ἔργον
ἐσθίω
εὑρίσκω
ἵστημι
καθώς
καρδία

b. Write the meaning of the grammatical terms:

active voice

passive voice

middle voice

deponent verbs

aorist tense

c. Explain the significance of the moods in Greek verbs.

| Mood | Significance |
|---|---|
| Indicative | |
| Subjunctive | |

Imperative

Infinitive

Participle

d. Make a complete sentence diagram of John 1:1:

Ἐν ἀρχῇ ἦν ὁ λόγος,
καὶ ὁ λόγος ἦν πρὸς τὸν θεόν,
καὶ θεὸς ἦν ὁ λόγος.

Remember that _____|_____ represents the subject and verb, that = ____ represents a predicate nominative, and that \ represents the modification of something. To show connection with a conjunction, use the symbol ⇓ and write the conjunction beside the arrow. (We will study this more in the next chapter.)

e. Finish the morphological study of your verse. Make sure you have all the key words analyzed, especially the verbs. Make sure you have labeled each Greek word as a noun, adjective, article, pronoun, verb, preposition, conjunction, or adverb. Write the root form of the verbs and give their tense, mood, voice, person, and number. Write the base form of the nouns, and indicate the case, number, and gender. Use your tools, such as *The New Linguistic and Exegetical Key*, or linguistic software such as *BibleWorks*, *Logos*, or the online *Greek New Testament*.

# LESSON 12

# SYNTAX AND CONJUNCTIONS

*In this lesson you will study conjunctions and the* **syntax** *(sentence structure) of complex sentences. You have already looked at some sentence structure as you made diagrams of simple sentences, but now you will look at* **complex** *sentences. When you finish the lesson, you will explain the structure of your text, write the conclusions of your linguistic study, and write your final translation of the text.*

1) Study of the original context
2) Linguistic analysis
      a) textual apparatus
      b) semantics
      c) morphology
      **d) syntax**

## 12.1 Conjunctions and complex syntax

A subject can have more than one part. In that case, the parts are united by a conjunction. For example, in the following sentence, "and" is a conjunction that unites the phrases "a man" and "his wife," making a complex subject.

The man **and** his wife go to church.

This sentence could be diagrammed in the following way:

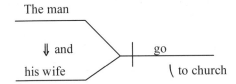

Conjunctions can also unite phrases such as the following:

The man works in the house **and** in the office.

The following diagram shows the relationships:

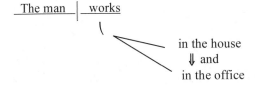

Definitions:
-A sentence is called *complex* when it has more than one clause.
-For our present purposes we will define a *clause* as a group of words that contains a verb and expresses an idea.
-In contrast with a clause, we will define a *phrase* as a group of words without a verb.

In a *complex* sentence, conjunctions unite the clauses.

The man reads the Bible, **but** he does not understand it.

The man | reads |→ the Bible

⇓ but

(the man) | does understand |→ it
\ not

The subject of the second clause is understood.

## 12.2 Syntax of complex sentences

As we saw above in our study of conjunctions, some sentences are composed of more than one clause. A clause must have a verb and must communicate an idea. There are independent clauses that stand by themselves, and there are dependent clauses that have no meaning alone. For example, in the sentence, "Peter bought a book because he wanted to learn Greek," the independent clause is "Peter bought a book," and the dependent clause is "because he wanted to learn Greek." If you read just the first clause by itself, it makes sense, but if you read the second clause alone, you realize that something is missing.

A clause can serve as the subject of another clause, or be part of a prepositional phrase. One clause can also be the direct object of another. For example, suppose that the sentence is:

Jesus said, "I am the good shepherd."

"Jesus" is the subject, "said" is the verb, and the direct object is the quote, which is another clause, "I am the good shepherd."

Jesus | said |→ [clause 2]

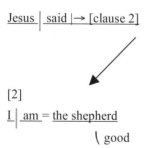

[2]
I | am = the shepherd
\ good

Let's look at another example: "Jesus came to the world because He wanted to save His people."

There are three verbs and three clauses:
Jesus *came* to the world
because He *wanted*
*to save* His people

"Jesus came to the world" is the main clause.

"Because He wanted" is a dependent clause using "because" to connect to the previous clause.

"To save His people" is another dependent clause that functions like the direct object of "wanted." It tells us what He wanted.

We might diagram it like this:

Jesus | came
    \ to the world

⇓  because

He | wanted |→ [clause 3]

[3]

    X | to save |→ His people

We put an "X" in the subject space in clause 3, because the infinitive "to save" does not have a subject.

**12.3 Syntax of John 3:16**

Now let's go back to our verse and analyze the syntax. The first step is to identify the main clause, and any dependent clauses. In each clause, we need to find the subject, verb, direct object, and indirect object, if any. Then we look for adjectives, adverbs, and prepositional phrases. Look at the example of John 3:16.

Clause #1 is:

Οὕτως γὰρ ἠγάπησεν ὁ θεὸς τὸν κόσμον,

The main clause of John 3:16 is "God loved the world" (ἠγάπησεν ὁ θεὸς τὸν κόσμον). "God" (ὁ θεὸς) is the subject, "loved" (ἠγάπησεν) is the verb, and "the world" (τὸν κόσμον) is the direct object (in accusative case). "So" (Οὕτως) is an adverb modifying "loved," and "for" (γὰρ) is a conjunction, connecting the idea with the previous verse.

The diagram is like this:

⇓γὰρ

ὁ θεὸς | ἠγάπησεν |→ τὸν κόσμον
    \ Οὕτως

101

Clause #2 is:

$$\H{\omega}\sigma\tau\epsilon\ \tau\grave{o}\nu\ \upsilon\acute{\iota}\grave{o}\nu\ \tau\grave{o}\nu\ \mu o\nu o\gamma\epsilon\nu\hat{\eta}\ \H{\epsilon}\delta\omega\kappa\epsilon\nu,$$

The word "that" (ὥστε) introduces a second clause that depends on the first: "He gave his one and only son" (τὸν υἱὸν τὸν μονογενῆ ἔδωκεν). The subject of this clause ("He") is contained within the verb in Greek and is understood to refer back to God. The verb is "gave" (ἔδωκεν), and "his one and only son" (τὸν υἱὸν τὸν μονογενῆ) is the direct object. Remember that "one and only" is actually a translation of one Greek word, μονογενῆ, which is an adjective that modifies "son." It literally means "one of a kind," and not "only begotten," as the King James translation puts it. It could be translated also "unique." The Greek does not really say "his son" but only "the son." However, it is clear that the verse is speaking about "His" son.

The diagram is like this:

⇓ ὥστε

(ὁ θεός) | ἔδωκεν | → τὸν υἱὸν
\ τὸν μονογενῆ

Clause #3

$$\H{\iota}\nu\alpha\ \pi\hat{\alpha}\varsigma\ \H{o}\ \pi\iota\sigma\tau\epsilon\acute{\upsilon}\omega\nu\ \epsilon\H{\iota}\varsigma\ \alpha\dot{\upsilon}\tau\grave{o}\nu\ \mu\grave{\eta}\ \dot{\alpha}\pi\acute{o}\lambda\eta\tau\alpha\iota\ \dot{\alpha}\lambda\lambda'\ \H{\epsilon}\chi\eta\ \zeta\omega\grave{\eta}\nu\ \alpha\grave{\iota}\acute{\omega}\nu\iota o\nu.$$

Now let's look at the third clause, "that whoever believes in him shall not perish but have eternal life." The word ἵνα ("that") is a conjunction that connects the clauses, indicating purpose. In Greek, ἵνα requires a verb in subjunctive mood. The subject is πᾶς ("all," "every one"), and the participle phrase ὁ πιστεύων εἰς αὐτόν ("believing in him") modifies the subject. There are two subjunctive verbs that follow ἵνα: ἀπόληται ("be destroyed") and ἔχη ("have"). The negation μὴ ("not") modifies the verb "be destroyed." A conjunction ἀλλ' ("but") connects the two verbs. "Life" (ζωὴν) is the direct object of "have," and "eternal" (αἰώνιον) is an adjective modifying "life."

The diagram is as follows:

⇓ ἵνα

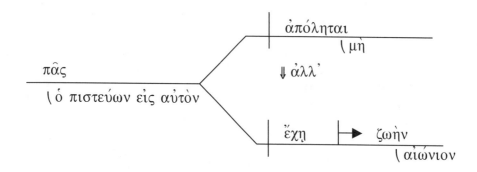

The complete diagram of John 3:16 is as follows:

⇓ γάρ

$\underline{\text{ὁ θεός} \mid \text{ἠγάπησεν} \mid\rightarrow \text{τὸν κόσμον}}$
$\quad\quad\quad \setminus \text{Οὕτως}$

⇓ ὥστε

$\underline{\text{(ὁ θεός)} \mid \text{ἔδωκεν} \mid\rightarrow \text{τὸν υἱὸν}}$
$\quad\quad\quad\quad \setminus \text{τὸν μονογενῆ}$

⇓ ἵνα

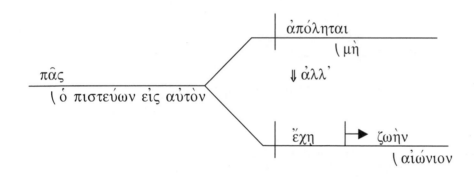

In English, the diagram of John 3:16 (translated more literally) looks like this:

⇓ For

<u>God</u> | <u>loved</u> |→ <u>the world</u>
          \ so

⇓ that

<u>(He)</u> | <u>gave</u> |→ <u>son</u>
          \ the only

⇓ in order that

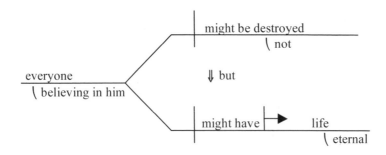

## 12.4 The use of *Logos* software to make sentence diagrams

The *Logos* program has a function that helps you make sentence diagrams easily.

1. Go to the menu and mark "file," "new," "sentence diagrams," and "OK."
2. Click "insert passage" and write the reference to the passage you wish to diagram, and choose the version you wish to use. We recommend the Greek version "Nestlé-Aland."
3. Now you can use the tools on the left to add symbols to the work space, indicating relationships such as subject, predicate, and direct object. Move the mouse over the symbol you wish to use, click the left mouse button, drag the symbol into the space, and release the button.
4. After placing the line symbols, you can move the words one at a time to put them in the appropriate place. Just highlight the word, click the left mouse button, move it to the proper place, and release the button.
5. To copy the whole diagram into your word processor, use the control key and click with the mouse on the different parts of the diagram until they are all highlighted in yellow. Then click on copy.
6. When you close the diagramming window, you must name the file in order to save it and use it again.

## 12.5 Conclusions from the linguistic study

After studying the structure of the text, you should stop a moment to reflect on what you have learned. For example, in John 3:16 we see that there is a sequence of relationships: God loved the world, and the result is that He gave His only Son. The purpose of giving His Son was so that those who believe in Him should not be destroyed, but that they might have eternal life. The basis of everything is God's love, His action is to give His Son, and the result is eternal life for believers. God does not simply give His Son as an example, but with the purpose of saving. The present tense of the participle "believe" indicates that faith in Christ should be a continuous thing, and not something that just happened once.

**EXERCISES**

a) Analyze the syntax of your verse (in Greek). Make a diagram of each sentence. Explain the structure. Identify the clauses by their subjects and verbs. If there is more than one clause, show how they relate to each other. Which is the main clause? Which are dependent? Identify any prepositional phrases. Find any conjunctions that connect clauses. There may be more than one way of describing the syntax of your verse. The main thing is to make an effort to understand how it all fits together.

b) Write down the conclusions of your linguistic study. Include any aspect that has especially caught your attention.

Finally:

c) Write your own final version of a translation of the text. Take into account what you have studied. Your translation may be different from the common versions, or it might be exactly the same. But now you are much more familiar with the verse and have your own idea of its meaning.

# LESSON 13

# ANALYSIS OF THE BIBLICAL AND THEOLOGICAL IMPLICATIONS

*In this lesson, you will learn to interpret the text biblically and theologically. When you finish the lesson, you will write down your own theological reflections on your verse.*

There are three aspects to this process:

a. Summarize the main message of the text in your own words.
b. Analyze the text biblically and theologically.
c. Read good commentaries on the passage.

## 13.1 Summary of the main message of the text

We have studied the original context of our verse, and we have done a linguistic analysis of it. Now is the moment to reflect and draw conclusions. Ask yourself, "What is the main point of the text?" We are not looking for applications yet, but seeking the principal message of the text. Think about how the first readers would have understood it. What did it mean for them?

For example, the main point of John 3:16 is that God has given His Son so that those who believe in Him might have eternal life. When Jesus spoke these words, the concept of *eternal life* may have been somewhat new to those who heard Him. The first readers must have struggled with the mystery of the Trinity, and marveled at how God could give His own Son to a sinful world. We should never lose our sense of wonder at the amazing message of the gospel!

## 13.2 Biblical and theological interpretation

Now we should address the theological and biblical issues.

a. Ask questions
If you are studying John 3:16, you might have questions such as: If the "world" is all of humanity, and if God loves the "world," why does He not save everybody? If God sent His Son to die for people to have "eternal life," why is not everybody saved? What does it really mean to "believe" in Jesus? What is "eternal life"?

b. Meditate
Try to understand the meaning of the verse in the context of the whole Bible. What are the theological questions that arise? Does your present understanding of the verse seem to contradict another Bible passage? Does it contradict another important doctrine? Try to harmonize it with the rest of Scripture. Examine any parallel passages again to see if they help you understand your text. Look for any other passages related to the topic. Think about the context of redemption. What does this text teach us about Jesus and salvation?

c. Read commentaries

You may wonder why we have waited until now to read commentaries. The reason is that we want you to discover on your own the meaning of the text before reading what others say. If you read the commentaries first, you will lose the fruit of original research. The commentaries can be gravely mistaken, and it might send you on the wrong path from the beginning, or the commentaries might just leave out some important aspects. We want you to become an authoritative expositor of the significance of the verse you are studying, and not simply to quote other authors.

However, now that you have already arrived at your own (at least tentative) conclusions, go ahead and read some commentaries and theological books to see what they say. Talk to a person that you trust and ask him or her to recommend good books. Remember always to keep Christ in the center of your thoughts and reflect on how your text fits in the plan of salvation. Jesus is "the way, the truth, and the life." Somehow all truth revolves around Him.

**EXERCISES**

1) Write a summary in your own words of the main message of your text.

"XX:XX (reference of your text) teaches that _____."

2) Analyze the biblical and theological implications of your text.

a. Write down your questions.

b. Meditate and write down your answers.

c. Read several good commentaries on your text and write down any important thoughts or new discoveries.

# LESSON 14

# APPLICATION TO THE PRESENT CONTEXT

*In this lesson, you will learn to make the application of the message of a biblical text in your own life and in the life of others in your context. When you finish, you will write down appropriate applications for your selected text.*

Making an application of a message is like moving to a new city. We need to get acquainted with the neighborhood, bring our furniture, and get installed in a new house. If you do not apply the message of a text, you still do not understand it properly. In the biblical sense, you do not really "know" the truth until you live it. This is where our studies become really significant and cease to be abstract reflections.

The two steps for application are:
    a. Reflect on our present context.
    b. Seek practical applications.

## 14.1 Reflections about the present context

We need to analyze the context in which we live: ourselves, our family, our work place, society in general. This exercise is somewhat subjective, and we have to be careful not to distort things. However, we need to analyze people around us. What do the news programs communicate? In order to better understand the present context, you should take some time to read magazines, newspapers, and Internet articles about the world we live in. What do the songs, the movies, and the television shows convey? What are the needs and concerns of people around us, in our church, or at our office? What are young people struggling with? What do the artists and philosophers have to say?

As we think of John 3:16, we may realize that many people have a pantheistic concept of God; they think God is one with nature, and that He does not exist apart from the material world. Others may consider God to be an impersonal force. Our text, on the contrary, shows that God is a personal loving God with emotions, and that He exists apart from His own creation.

Some people have an erroneous concept of faith. Some think it is enough to believe that God exists, or that Jesus was a wonderful man. Others think it means an irrational blind leap against reason. Even some in the church are confused, thinking it is sufficient to have "accepted Christ" by going forward in an evangelistic service. While many people are truly saved in a moment like that, the act of raising your hand or going forward does not necessarily mean you have true saving faith.

As for the concept of eternal life, many people in our day have accepted an oriental concept of reincarnation. Others believe that when you die, there is nothing more. John 3:16 and the surrounding verses indicate that some people will have eternal life and others will perish.

### 14.2 Practical applications

Finally, we must look for concrete practical applications for our day. All of our efforts to analyze the passage should end with some kind of spiritual blessing, with some positive change. What should I do to respond to the truths of this text? Here we need the Lord's special help, and we must ask for His guidance in prayer.

To apply John 3:16, maybe we will see the need to share the gospel with those who are on the road to destruction. Possibly the text has filled me with joy and I wish to praise the Lord for His love and mercy. I should also follow God's example of sacrificial love.

### EXERCISES

Follow the steps of application for your selected text.

1) Write down important aspects of the context you live in that are related to the message of your text. Take some time to read magazines, newspapers, and Internet articles about the current events, in order to capture the signs of the times.

2) Look for practical concrete applications. What should I do as a result of my exegesis?

Write something like this: Since John 3:16 (substitute the reference for your text) teaches that
_____ (the main message of the text), I am going to
_____ (the main application)."

# LESSON 15

# THE WRITTEN EXEGESIS REPORT

*Now you will learn how to write the results of your exegesis in the form of a report, and you will perform the task, using the studies of your selected text.*

This is like inviting your friends to a new house that you have built. What a joy to show the fruit of your labors! After analyzing a passage, you can't resist sharing the results with others!

## 15.1 The outline

We recommend using the steps of the exegesis process for the titles of your report. You just need to add an introduction and a conclusion.

Introduction
I. Analysis of the original context
    A. The historical context
    B. The literary context
    C. The redemptive context
II. Linguistic analysis
    A. The textual apparatus
    B. Semantics
    C. Morphology
    D. Syntax
III. Analysis of the biblical and theological implications
    A. The main message of the text
    B. Biblical and theological interpretation
IV. Application in the present context
    A. Analysis of the present context
    B. Concrete applications
Conclusion

## 15.2 The introduction

The introduction should catch the attention of the reader. It might call attention to some difficulty in the interpretation of the text, or to a theological problem that arises from the text. You can probably share the questions you had at the very beginning, the concerns that led you to pick the text for study. The introduction should be brief, no more than a page.

## 15.3 The body

In the body of the report, you will present the results of your study from each step of exegesis. You can't include all the information, but rather the most significant things you have learned, information related to the questions you have and to the application you will make. The complete report should focus on how you are led to the main application. The reader should come to the end convinced that your application is valid because your interpretation of the passage is correct. The body of the report should be 8–10 pages long.

### 15.4 The conclusion

In the conclusion, you should summarize the most important aspect of the exegesis and make an exhortation to put into practice the central message of the text. You could finish with an illustration that highlights the importance of the passage, telling a story or giving an example. The conclusion should also be brief, one or two pages.

### 15.5 Form

While the content is the most important aspect of the report, the form makes the content more attractive. Be careful to use good spelling and grammar. Use the automatic spelling and grammar checker of your word processor, if possible. The style should be serious, but also interesting. Make it clear and easy to follow. Don't forget to include footnotes where you have used ideas from another source, or if you have quoted another author. At the end of the report, include a bibliography with all the sources you have used in your exegetical study: *The New Linguistic and Exegetical Key*, software, lexicons, commentaries, and so forth.

### 15.6 The final revision

Polish your exegesis report until it is publishable:

- Be very strict with yourself about spelling, grammar, and style.
- Don't forget the footnotes and bibliography.
- Try to organize the report around one main point. Your passage probably points to several fascinating issues. However, you can't deal thoroughly with everything. Imagine that you are preaching a sermon or teaching a Bible study on the passage. What would your main point be? What would your main application be? Whatever that point is, try to make that point the unifying theme of the report.
- Review your report several times. Correct errors, take out insignificant information, and explain important points more clearly.
- Put yourself in the reader's place. Will it be clear to him or her? Try reading it out loud. Where you stumble on the words, rewrite it until it flows. If possible, ask a friend to read it and give you suggestions.

### EXERCISE

Prepare your exegesis report, following the instructions of this lesson. Make an outline, and write the important things to include under each section. Think about ideas for the introduction and the conclusion. Reflect on possible illustrations. Review all the notes you have been taking. As you review the outline with initial sketches of points to make, take out any information that seems irrelevant, and add other points that are missing. Put yourself in the place of a person who has not studied your text, and try to make your report interesting and easy for the reader to understand. Keep the focus on your main point.

# LESSON 16

# GREEK: REVIEW

*In this lesson, you will review all the Greek in the lessons of this course. When you finish, you will be prepared to give the meaninsg of a list of vocabulary taken from the lessons, you will be able to explain the meanings of key grammatical concepts, you will be able to identify parts of sentences, identify the forms of some Greek words, and translate some sentences that you have already learned in the lessons.*

Review all the exercises to make sure that you know the material. If you can do the exercises, you should do well on the exam. May the Lord bless you as you continue to study His Word and minister to others!

# ANSWERS TO EXERCISES

**Lessons 1–2**
The answers for these lessons will vary from student to student, according to the text he or she selects.

**Lesson 3**
a. (self evaluation)

b.

| | | |
|---|---|---|
| γ | gamma | g |
| δ | delta | d |
| α | alpha | a |
| ω | omega | ō |
| ζ | zeta | z |
| σ | sigma | s |
| ς | final sigma | s |
| ρ | rho | r |
| τ | tau | t |
| φ | phi | ph |
| ξ | xi | x |
| ψ | psi | <u>ps</u> |
| β | beta | b |
| ν | nu | n |
| μ | mu | m |
| λ | lambda | l |
| κ | kappa | k |
| χ | chi | <u>ch</u> |
| θ | theta | <u>th</u> |
| ι | iota | i |
| ο | omicron | o |
| υ | upsilon | u |
| η | eta | ê |
| ε | epsilon | e |
| π | pi | p |

c. (self evaluation)

d.

| | |
|---|---|
| Κ | kappa |
| Λ | lambda |
| Μ | mu |
| Ν | nu |
| Σ | sigma |
| Ρ | rho |
| Ε | epsilon |
| Τ | tau |
| Θ | theta |
| Ι | iota |
| Π | pi |
| Α | alpha |
| Δ | delta |
| Β | beta |
| Φ | phi |
| Γ | gamma |
| Η | eta |
| Ξ | xi |
| Ζ | zeta |
| Ο | omicron |
| Υ | upsilon |
| Χ | chi |
| Ψ | psi |
| Ω | omega |

e.

| | |
|---|---|
| ἀγαπάω | love, like |
| ἀδελφός | brother |
| ἀνήρ | man, husband |
| ἄνθρωπος | man, human |
| γάρ | because |
| εἰμί | I am |
| ἔχω | I have |
| ἔχει | he or she has |
| ζωή | life |
| θεός | God |
| ἵνα | in order that, that |
| κόσμος | world |
| λέγω | I say, I speak |
| λέγει | he or she says, speaks |
| λόγος | word |

f.

| | |
|---|---|
| κύριος | Lord, master |
| ποιέω | I do, I make |

**Lessons 4–7**

The exercises of these lessons, as in all exercises of exegesis, have varied answers according to the Bible text that the student has selected. At the end of the course, the student will prepare an exegesis report that will show the results of his or her study.

**Lesson 8**

a.

| | Masc. | Fem. | Neutral |
|---|---|---|---|
| Singular | | | |
| Nom. | ὁ | ἡ | τό |
| Gen. | τοῦ | τῆς | τοῦ |
| Dat. | τῷ | τῇ | τῷ |
| Acc. | τόν | τήν | τό |
| Plural | | | |
| Nom. | οἱ | αἱ | τά |
| Gen. | τῶν | τῶν | τῶν |
| Dat. | τοῖς | ταῖς | τοῖς |
| Acc. | τούς | τάς | τά |

b.  
nominative case: subject  
genitive case: possession  
dative case: indirect object  
accusative case: direct object  
vocative case: direct address

c.

| | Gender | Number | Case |
|---|---|---|---|
| οἱ ἀδελφοί | masc | pl | nom |
| τοῦ ἀδελφοῦ | masc | sing | gen |
| τῶν ἀδελφῶν | masc | pl | gen |
| τὸ τέκνον | neut | sing | nom or accus |
| τὰ τέκνα | neut | pl | nom or accus |
| τοῖς τέκνοις | neut | pl | dat |
| τῇ γραφῇ | fem | sing | dat |
| τῶν γραφῶν | fem | pl | gen |
| ταῖς γραφαῖς | fem | pl | dat |
| τῆς γραφῆς | fem | sing | gen |

d.

| | |
|---|---|
| ἀλλά | but |
| βλέπω | I see |
| γῆ | earth, land |
| γραφή | writing |
| ἐστὶ | it, he, or she is |
| ἡμέρα | day |
| καί | and |
| κύριος | Lord |
| μαθητῆς | student, disciple |
| ὄνομα | name |
| ὁ, ἡ, τό | the |
| ὅτι | that, because |
| πᾶς, πᾶσα, πᾶν | all, every |
| ποιέω | I do, I make |
| τέκνον | child |
| υἱός | son |

e.

1) The teacher sees the student.
        S     V      DO

2) The student has a book.
        S     V      DO

3) The teacher bought me a book.
        S     V      IO    DO

4) The student is the brother of the man.
        S     V     PrNom   Poss

5) The student read the book to the teacher.
        S     V      DO    IO

6) The brother is the teacher of the child.
        S     V     PrNom   Poss

7) ὁ ἄνθρωπος ἔχει ἀδελφόν.
     S      V    DO
   (Nom)      (Accus)
  The man has a brother.

8) ὁ ἀδελφὸς λέγει λόγον.
     S      V    DO
   (Nom)      (Accus)
  The brother says a word.

9) ὁ ἄνθρωπος λέγει λόγον τῷ ἀδελφῷ.
     S      V    DO    IO
   (Nom)      (Accus)  (Dat)
  The man says a word to the brother.

10) ὁ ἀδελφός ἐστιν ὁ μαθητῆς.
     S     V    PrNom
   (Nom)      (Nom)
  The brother is the disciple.

11) τὸν ἄνθρωπον βλέπει ὁ κύριος.
     DO      V    S
   (Accus)      (Nom)
  The Lord sees the man.

12) βλέπω τὸ τέκνον τοῦ ἀδελφοῦ.
     V      DO    Poss
        (Accus)   (Gen)
  I see the child of the brother.

13) τὴν γραφὴν ποίει ὁ υἱός.
     DO      V    S
   (Accus)      (Nom)
  The son makes the writing.

14) ὁ ἀδελφὸς ἔχει τὴν γραφὴν τοῦ κυρίου.
     S      V    DO    Poss
   (Nom)      (Accus)  (Gen)
  The brother has the writing of the Lord.

15) τῷ τέκνῳ λέγει λόγον ὁ κύριος.
     IO      V    DO    S
   (Dat)      (Accus)  (Nom)
  The Lord says a word to the child.

16) ὁ υἱὸς λέγει ὄνομα τῷ ἀδελφῷ.
    S     V    DO     IO
  (Nom)     (Accus)    (Dat)
The son says a name to the brother.

17) τῷ ἀδελφῷ λέγει ὄνομα ὁ υἱός.
    IO     V    DO     S
  (Dat)      (Accus)   (Nom)
To the brother the son says a name.
(or, The son says a name to the brother.)

f.

1)    ὁ ἄνθρωπος | ἔχει → ἀδελφόν.

2)    ὁ ἀδελφός | ἐστιν = ὁ μαθητῆς.

## Lesson 9
a.

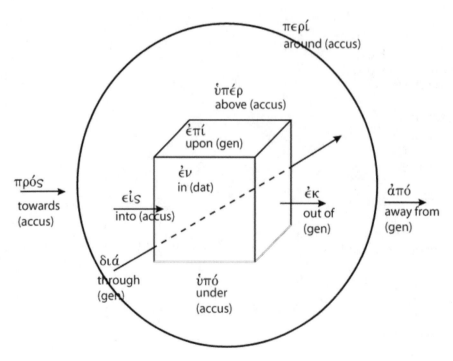

120

b.

| | |
|---|---|
| ἅγιος | holy |
| αἰών | age, eon, epoch |
| αἰώνιος | eternal |
| αὐτός, αὐτή, αὐτό | the same, he himself, she herself |
| γινώσκω | I know |
| γυνή | woman, wife |
| δίδωμι | I give |
| δύναμαι | I can |
| ἐγώ | I |
| ἐκεῖνος | that |
| ἔρχομαι | I come, I go |
| ἐξέρχομαι | I leave |
| ἤ | or |
| κατά | against, according to, during |
| λαλέω | I speak |
| μή | no |
| μόνον | only |
| νῦν | now |
| οὐ | no |
| πιστεύω | I believe |
| σύ | you |
| οὐρανός | heaven |
| οὗτος, αὕτη, τοῦτο | this |
| οὕτως | thus |

c.

1) The <u>tall</u> man bought a <u>good</u> book <u>in</u> the bookstore that <u>he</u> <u>often</u> visited.
     Adj          Adj     Prep               Pron Adv

2) <u>She</u> could <u>not</u> read the <u>excellent</u> book, because <u>he</u> did <u>not</u> bring <u>it</u> <u>from</u> the office.
   Pron      Adv         Adj              Pron  Adv  Pron Prep

3) <u>He</u> went <u>from</u> the office <u>to</u> the <u>beautiful</u> mountains <u>without</u> <u>her</u>.
   Pron     Prep         Prep     Adj          Prep    Pron

4) The <u>good</u> teacher teaches <u>faithfully</u> <u>in</u> the church.
      Adj               Adv  Prep

5) <u>She</u> <u>deeply</u> loves the <u>kind</u> man.
   Pron  Adv         Adj

6) ὁ ἀνὴρ ὁ <u>ἅγιος</u> λεγεῖ <u>νῦν</u> <u>ἐν</u> τῇ γῇ.
             Adj       Adv Prep

The holy man speaks now on the earth.

7) ὁ ἀνὴρ τοῦ θεοῦ ἐστιν <u>ἅγιος</u> <u>ἐπὶ</u> τῆς γῆς.
                  Adj   Prep

The man of God is holy on the earth.

8) ἡ γυνὴ ἡ <u>ἅγια</u> ἔρχεται <u>νῦν</u> <u>εἰς</u> τὸν κύριον <u>ἡμῶν</u>.
        Adj         Adv Prep           Pron

The holy woman comes now to our Lord.

9) δίδωμι <u>οὕτως</u> <u>αὐτῇ</u> τὸν λόγον τὸν <u>ἅγιον</u>.
        Adv   Pron             Adj

I give thus to her the holy word.

10) ἐξέρχομαι <u>ἐκ</u> τῆς γῆς <u>εἰς</u> τὸν οὐρανόν.
         Prep        Prep

I leave from the earth to heaven.

d.

<u>ὁ λόγος</u> | <u>ἦν</u>
          ( Ἐν ἀρχῇ

(The phrase "in the beginning" tells us *when* the Word *existed*.)

e. (Answers vary according to verse.)

**Lesson 10**

a.

| | |
|---|---|
| 1 sing | –ω, –α, –ον |
| 2 sing | –ς |
| 3 sing | –ει, –ε, –εν |
| | |
| 1 plural | –μεν |
| 2 plural | –τε |
| 3 plural | –σι(ν), σαν, –ον |

b.

**present**
simple action in the present, or progressive action at present time

**imperfect**
continuous action in the past

**future**
future action

**aorist**

action seen in its totality (sometimes, not always, in the past)

**perfect**

action *completed* in the past, whose effects continue now

**pluperfect**

past action previous to another past action

c.

| | |
|---|---|
| 1 sing | λύω |
| 2 sing | λύεις |
| 3 sing | λύει |
| | |
| 1 plural | λύομεν |
| 2 plural | λύετε |
| 3 plural | λύουσι(ν) |

d.

| | Pres | Imp | Fut | Aor | Perf | Plup |
|---|---|---|---|---|---|---|
| Augment | | ε | | ε | | ε |
| Reduplication | | | | | R | R |
| Addition to the root | | | σ | σ | κ | κ |

e.

| | | |
|---|---|---|
| V | = | present |
| ε V | = | imperfect |
| V σ | = | future |
| ε V σ | = | aorist |
| R V κ | = | perfect |
| ε R V κ | = | pluperfect |

f.

| | |
|---|---|
| ἀποστέλλω | I send |
| θέλω | I desire |
| καλέω | I call, I invite |
| λαμβάνω | I take, I receive |
| λύω | I loose, I free |
| μετά | with (when used with genitive) |
| | after (when used with accusative) |
| οὖν | then |
| πατήρ | father |
| πίστις | faith, belief |
| πνεῦμα | spirit |
| πολύς | much, many |
| σῶμα | body |
| φωνή | voice |

g.

| | Tense | Person | Number | Translation |
|---|---|---|---|---|
| λύω | pres | 1 | sing | I loose |
| λύει | pres | 3 | sing | he looses |
| λύομεν | pres | 1 | pl | we loose |
| λύουσι | pres | 3 | pl | they loose |
| ἐλύομεν | imperf | 1 | pl | we were loosing |
| ἐλύετε | imperf | 2 | pl | you were loosing |
| λύσει | fut | 3 | sing | he shall loose |
| λύσουσιν | fut | 3 | pl | they shall loose |
| ἔλυσας | aorist | 2 | sing | you loosed |
| ἐλύσαμεν | aorist | 1 | pl | we loosed |

h.

$$\underline{\text{ὁ λόγος} \mid \text{ἦν}}$$
$$\text{\textbackslash πρὸς τὸν θεόν}$$

i. (Answers will vary according to the verse.)

**Lesson 11**
a.

| | |
|---|---|
| ἄγγελος | messenger, angel |
| ἁμαρτία | sin |
| βασιλεία | kingdom |
| γίνομαι | become |
| γράφω | write |
| δόξα | glory |
| ἔθνος | nation, ethnic group, gentile |
| ἔργον | work |
| ἐσθίω | eat |
| εὑρίσκω | find |
| ἵστημι | stand |
| καθώς | as, just as |
| καρδία | heart |

b.

| | |
|---|---|
| active voice | the subject acts |
| passive voice | the subject receives the action (or, is acted upon) |
| middle voice | the subject is indirectly acted upon |
| deponent verbs | verbs that have the form of middle or passive voice, but the meaning of active voice |
| aorist tense | sees the action in its totality |

c.

| Mood | Significance |
|---|---|
| Indicative | indicates something |
| Subjunctive | shows probability, purpose, contrary to reality |
| Imperative | command |
| Infinitive | unlimited (used grammatically as a noun) |
| Participle | similar to a participle in English (used grammatically as an adjective) |

d.

$\underline{\text{ὁ λόγος}}\ |\ \underline{\hat{\text{ἦν}}}$
                ( Ἐν ἀρχῇ

⇓ καὶ

$\underline{\text{ὁ λόγος}}\ |\ \underline{\hat{\text{ἦν}}}$
            \ πρὸς τὸν θεόν

⇓ καὶ

$\underline{\text{ὁ λόγος}}|\ \underline{\hat{\text{ἦν}}}\ =\ \underline{\text{θεὸς}}$

e. (Answers will vary according to the verse.)

**Lessons 12–18**

(Answers will vary according to the passage studied.)

# APPENDIX

**NOUNS**

ὁ ἀδελφός (*ho adelphós*) the brother
**Singular**

| | | |
|---|---|---|
| N. | ὁ ἀδελφός | the brother |
| G. | τοῦ ἀδελφοῦ | of the brother |
| D. | τῷ ἀδελφῷ | for the brother |
| A. | τὸν ἀδελφόν | the brother |
| V. | — ἀδελφέ | Brother! |

**Plural**

| | | |
|---|---|---|
| N. | οἱ ἀδελφοί | the brothers |
| G. | τῶν ἀδελφῶν | of the brothers |
| D. | τοῖς ἀδελφοῖς | for the brothers |
| A. | τοὺς ἀδελφούς | the brothers |
| V. | — ἀδελφοί | Brothers! |

τὸ τέκνον (*to téknon*) the child
**Singular**

| | | |
|---|---|---|
| N. | τὸ τέκνον | the child |
| G. | τοῦ τέκνου | of the child |
| D. | τῷ τέκνῳ | for the child |
| A. | τὸ τέκνον | the child |
| V. | — τέκνον | Child! |

**Plural**

| | | |
|---|---|---|
| N. | τὰ τέκνα | the children |
| G. | τῶν τέκνων | of the children |
| D. | τοῖς τέκνοις | for the children |
| A. | τὰ τέκνα | the children |
| V. | — τέκνα | Children! |

## ἡ γραφή  (*hê graphê*) the writing

**Singular**

| | | |
|---|---|---|
| N. | ἡ γραφή | the writing |
| G. | τῆς γραφῆς | of the writing |
| D. | τῇ γραφῇ | for the writing |
| A. | τὴν γραφήν | the writing |
| V. | — γραφή | Writing! |

**Plural**

| | | |
|---|---|---|
| N. | αἱ γραφαί | the writings |
| G. | τῶν γραφῶν | of the writings |
| D. | ταῖς γραφαῖς | for the writings |
| A. | τὰς γραφάς | the writings |
| V. | — γραφαί | Writings! |

## ἄνθρωπος

**Singular**

| | |
|---|---|
| N. | ἄνθρωπος |
| G. | ἀνθρώπου |
| D. | ἀνθρώπῳ |
| A. | ἄνθρωπον |
| V. | ἄνθρωπε |

**Plural**

| | |
|---|---|
| N.V. | ἄνθρωποι |
| G. | ἀνθρώπων |
| D. | ἀνθρώποις |
| A. | ἀνθρώπους |

## καρδία

**Singular**

| | |
|---|---|
| N.V. | καρδία |
| G. | καρδίας |
| D. | καρδίᾳ |
| A. | καρδίαν |

**Plural**

| | |
|---|---|
| N.V. | καρδίαι |
| G. | καρδιῶν |
| D. | καρδίαις |
| A. | καρδίας |

## PERSONAL PRONOUNS

| 1st person sing. | 1 pl. | 2nd person sing. | 2 pl. |
|---|---|---|---|
| ἐγώ | ἡμεῖς | σύ | ὑμεῖς |
| ἐμοῦ / μου | ἡμῶν | σοῦ | ὑμῶν |
| ἐμοί / μοι | ἡμῖν | σοί | ὑμῖν |
| ἐμέ / με | ἡμᾶς | σέ | ὑμᾶς |

**3rd person (he, she, they)**

| Masculine | Feminine | Neutral |
|---|---|---|
| **Singular** | | |
| αὐτός | αὐτή | αὐτό |
| αὐτοῦ | αὐτῆς | αὐτοῦ |
| αὐτῷ | αὐτῇ | αὐτῷ |
| αὐτόν | αὐτήν | αὐτό |
| **Plural** | | |
| αὐτοί | αὐταί | αὐτά |
| αὐτῶν | αὐτῶν | αὐτῶν |
| αὐτοῖς | αὐταῖς | αὐτοῖς |
| αὐτούς | αὐτάς | αὐτά |

## THE DEFINITE ARTICLE

| **Singular** | | |
|---|---|---|
| **Masculine** | **Feminine** | **Neutral** |
| ὁ | ἡ | τό |
| τοῦ | τῆς | τοῦ |
| τῷ | τῇ | τῷ |
| τόν | τήν | τό |

| **Plural** | | |
|---|---|---|
| **Masculine** | **Feminine** | **Neutral** |
| οἱ | αἱ | τά |
| τῶν | τῶν | τῶν |
| τοῖς | ταῖς | τοῖς |
| τούς | τάς | τά |

## PARTICIPLES

The forms of the participle of πιστεύω in present tense singular:

|  | Masculine | Feminine | Neutral |
|---|---|---|---|
| **Singular** |  |  |  |
| N. | πιστεύων | πιστεύουσα | πιστεῦον |
| G. | πιστεύοντος | πιστευούσης | πιστεύοντος |
| D. | πιστεύοντι | πιστευούση | πιστεύοντι |
| A. | πιστεύοντα | πιστεύουσαν | πιστεῦον |
| **Plural** |  |  |  |
| N. | πιστεύοντες | πιστεύουσαι | πιστεύοντα |
| G. | πιστευόντων | πιστευουσῶν | πιστευόντων |
| D. | πιστεύουσι | πιστευούσαις | πιστεύουσι |
| A. | πιστεύοντας | πιστευούσας | πιστεύοντα |

## ANALYSIS OF THE VERB IN INDICATIVE MOOD

|  | Pres | Imp | Fut | Aor | Perf | Plup |
|---|---|---|---|---|---|---|
| Augment |  | ε |  | ε |  | ε |
| Reduplication |  |  |  |  | R | R |
| Addition to the root |  |  | σ | σ | κ | κ |

| | |
|---|---|
| V | = present |
| ε V | = imperfect |
| V σ | = future |
| ε V σ | = aorist |
| R V κ | = perfect |
| ε R V κ | = pluperfect |

## PARADIGM OF THE REGULAR VERB, λύω, INDICATIVE MOOD

| | Pres Act | Pres M/P | Impf Act | Impf M/P | Fut Act | Fut M | Aor Act | Aor M |
|---|---|---|---|---|---|---|---|---|
| **Indicative** | λύω<br>I loose | λύομαι<br>I loose myself / I am loosed | ἔλυον<br>I was loosing | ἐλυόμην<br>I was loosing myself / I was being loosed | λύσω<br>I shall loose | λύσομαι<br>I shall loose myself | ἔλυσα<br>I loosed | ἐλυσάμην<br>I loosed myself |
| | λύεις<br>you loose | λύῃ<br>you loose yourself / you are loosed | ἔλυες<br>you were loosing | ἐλύου<br>you were loosing yourself / you were being loosed | λύσεις<br>you shall loose | λύσῃ<br>you shall loose yourself | ἔλυσας<br>you loosed | ἐλύσω<br>you loosed yourself |
| | λύει<br>he looses | λύεται<br>he looses himself / he is loosed | ἔλυε(ν)<br>he was loosing | ἐλύετο<br>he was loosing himself / he was being loosed | λύσει<br>he shall loose | λύσεται<br>he shall loose himself | ἔλυσε(ν)<br>he loosed | ἐλύσατο<br>he loosed himself |
| | λύομεν<br>we loose | λυόμεθα<br>we loose ourselves / we are loosed | ἐλύομεν<br>we were loosing | ἐλυόμεθα<br>we were loosing ourselves / we were being loosed | λύσομεν<br>we shall loose | λυσόμεθα<br>we shall loose ourselves | ἐλύσαμεν<br>we loosed | ἐλυσάμεθα<br>we loosed ourselves |
| | λύετε<br>you loose | λύεσθε<br>you loose yourselves / you are loosed | ἐλύετε<br>you were loosing | ἐλύεσθε<br>you were loosing yourselves / you were being loosed | λύσετε<br>you shall loose | λύσεσθε<br>you shall loose yourselves | ἐλύσατε<br>you loosed | ἐλύσασθε<br>you loosed yourselves |
| | λύουσι(ν)<br>they loose | λύονται<br>they loose themselves / they are loosed | ἔλυον<br>they were loosing | ἐλύοντο<br>they were loosing themselves / they were being loosed | λύσουσι(ν)<br>they shall loose | λύσονται<br>they shall loose themselves | ἔλυσαν<br>they loosed | ἐλύσαντο<br>they loosed themselves |

## SUBJUNCTIVE MOOD

| Present Active | Present M/P | Aorist Active | Aorist Middle | Aorist Passive |
|---|---|---|---|---|
| λύω<br>I might loose | λύωμαι<br>I might loose myself | λύσω<br>I might loose | λύσωμαι<br>I might loose myself | λυθῶ<br>I might be loosed |
| λύῃς<br>you might loose | λύῃ<br>you might loose yourself | λύσῃς<br>you might loose | λύσῃ<br>you might loose yourself | λυθῇς<br>you might be loosed |
| λύῃ<br>he/she might loose | λύηται<br>he/she might loose himself/herself | λύσῃ<br>he/she might loose | λύσηται<br>he/she might loose himself/herself | λυθῇ<br>he/she might be loosed |
| λύωμεν<br>we might loose | λυώμεθα<br>we might loose ourselves | λύσωμεν<br>we might loose | λυσώμεθα<br>we might loose ourselves | λυθῶμεν<br>we might be loosed |
| λύητε<br>you might loose | λύησθε<br>you might loose yourselves | λύσητε<br>you might loose | λύσησθε<br>you might loose yourselves | λυθῆτε<br>you might be loosed |
| λύωσι(ν)<br>they might loose | λύωνται<br>they might loose themselves | λύσωσι(ν)<br>they might loose | λύσωνται<br>they might loose themselves | λυθῶσι(ν)<br>they might be loosed |

## IMPERATIVE AND INFINITIVE MOODS

| | Pres Act | Pres M/P | Aor Act | Aor Middle | Aor Passive |
|---|---|---|---|---|---|
| **Impv** | λῦε<br>Loose! | λύο<br>Loose yourself! / Be loosed! | λῦσον<br>Loose! | λῦσαι<br>Loose yourself! | λύθητι<br>Be loosed! |
| | λυέτω<br>May he loose! | λυέσθω<br>May he loose himself! / May he be loosed! | λυσάτω<br>May he loose! | λυσάσθω<br>May he loose himself! | λυθήτω<br>May he be loosed! |
| | λύετε<br>Loose! | λύεσθε<br>May you loose yourselves / May you be loosed! | λύσατε<br>Loose! | λύσασθε<br>May you loose yourselves! | λύθητε<br>May you be loosed! |
| | λυέτωσαν<br>May they loose! | λυέσθωσαν<br>May they loose themselves! / May they be loosed! | λυσάτωσαν<br>May they loose! | λυσάσθωσαν<br>May they loose themselves! | λυθήτωσαν<br>May they be loosed! |
| **Inf** | λύειν<br>to loose | λύεσθαι<br>to loose themselves/ to be loosed | λῦσαι<br>to loose | λύσασθαι<br>to loose oneself | λυθῆναι<br>to be loosed |

**PARTICIPLE MOOD**

|   | Pres Act | Pres M/P | Fut Act | Fut Middle | Aor Act | Aor Middle | Aor Pass |
|---|----------|----------|---------|------------|---------|------------|----------|
| **M** | λύων<br>loosing | λυόμενος<br>loosing himself | λύσων<br>going to loose | λυσόμενος<br>going to loose himself | λύσας<br>loosing | λυσάμενος<br>loosing himself | λυθείς<br>being loosed |
| **F** | λύουσα<br>loosing | λυομένη<br>loosing herself | λύσουσα<br>going to loose | λυσομένη<br>going to loose herself | λύσασα<br>loosing | λυσαμένη<br>loosing herself | λυθεῖσα<br>being loosed |
| **N** | λῦον<br>loosing | λυόμενον<br>loosing itself | λῦσον<br>going to loose | λυσόμενον<br>going to loose itself | λῦσαν<br>loosing | λυσάμενον<br>loosing itself | λυθέν<br>being loosed |

## PERFECT and PLUPERFECT Tense, plus AORIST and FUTURE PASSIVE
(Indicative, Subjunctive, Imperative, Infinitive, and Participle Moods)

| | Perf Act | Plupf Act | Perf M/P | Plupf M/P | Aor Pas | Fut Pas |
|---|---|---|---|---|---|---|
| **Indicative** | λέλυκα<br>I have loosed | ἐλελύκειν<br>I had loosed | λέλυμαι<br>I have loosed myself / I have been loosed | ἐλελύμην<br>I had loosed myself / I had been loosed | ἐλύθην<br>I was loosed | λυθήσομαι<br>I shall be loosed |
| | λέλυκας | ἐλελύκεις | λέλυσαι | ἐλέλυσο | ἐλύθης | λυθήσῃ |
| | λέλυκε(ν) | ἐλελύκει | λέλυται | ἐλέλυτο | ἐλύθη | λυθήσεται |
| | λελύκαμεν | ἐλελύκειμεν | λελύμεθα | ἐλελύμεθα | ἐλύθημεν | λυθησόμεθα |
| | λελύκατε | ἐλελύκειτε | λέλυσθε | ἐλέλυσθε | ἐλύθητε | λυθήσεσθε |
| | λελύκασι(ν) | ἐλελύκεισαν | λέλυνται | ἐλέλυντο | ἐλύθησαν | λυθήσονται |
| **Subjunctive** | λελύκω<br>I might have loosed | | | | λυθῶ<br>I might be loosed | |
| | λελύκῃς | | | | λυθῇς | |
| | λελύκῃ | | | | λυθῇ | |
| | λελύκωμεν | | | | λυθῶμεν | |
| | λελύκητε | | | | λυθῆτε | |
| | λελύκωσι(ν) | | | | λυθῶσι(ν) | |
| **Impv** | | | | | λύθητι<br>Be loosed! | |
| | | | | | λυθήτω | |
| | | | | | λύθητε | |
| | | | | | λυθήτωσαν | |
| **Inf** | λελυκέναι<br>to have loosed | | λελύσθαι<br>to have loosed oneself | | λυθῆναι<br>to be loosed | λυθήσεσθαι<br>having been loosed |
| **Ptc** | λελυκώς<br>having loosed | | λελυμένος<br>having loosed himself / having been loosed | | λυθείς<br>being loosed | λυθησόμενος<br>being about to be loosed |
| | λελυκυῖα | | λελυμένη | | λυθεῖσα | λυθησομένη |
| | λελυκός | | λελυμένον | | λυθέν | λυθησόμενον |

# SECOND AORIST OF βάλλω

|  | Active Voice | Middle Voice |
|---|---|---|
| **Indicative** | ἔβαλον | ἐβαλόμην |
|  | ἔβαλες | ἐβάλου |
|  | ἔβαλε | ἐβάλετο |
|  | ἐβάλομεν | ἐβαλόμεθα |
|  | ἐβάλετε | ἐβάλεσθε |
|  | ἔβαλον | ἐβάλοντο |
| **Subjunctive** | βάλω | βάλωμαι |
|  | βάλῃς | βάλῃ |
|  | βάλῃ | βάληται |
|  | βάλωμεν | βαλώμεθα |
|  | βάλητε | βάλησθε |
|  | βάλωσι | βάλωνται |
| **Impv** | βάλε | βάλου |
|  | βαλέτω | βαλέσθω |
|  | βάλετε | βάλεσθε |
|  | βαλέτωσαν | βαλέσθωσαν |
| **Inf** | βαλεῖν | βαλέσθαι |
| **Ptc** | βαλών | βαλόμενος |
|  | βαλοῦσα | βαλομένη |
|  | βαλόν | βαλόμενον |

## εἰμί (I am)

| | Present | Imperfect | Future |
|---|---|---|---|
| **Indicative** | εἰμί | ἤμην | ἔσομαι |
| | εἶ | ἦς | ἔσῃ |
| | ἐστί(ν) | ἦν | ἔσται |
| | ἐσμέν | ἦμεν | ἐσόμεθα |
| | ἐστέ | ἦτε | ἔσεσθε |
| | εἰσί | ἦσαν | ἔσονται |
| **Subjunctive** | ὦ | | |
| | ἦς | | |
| | ἦ | | |
| | ὦμεν | | |
| | ἦτε | | |
| | ὦσι(ν) | | |
| **Impv** | ἴσθι | | |
| | ἔστω | | |
| | ἔστε | | |
| | ἔστωσαν | | |
| **Inf** | εἶναι | | |
| **Ptc** | ὤν | | |
| | οὖσα | | |
| | ὄν | | |

## PRINCIPLE PARTS OF COMMON VERBS

| Present Act or Mid | Future Act or Mid | Aorist Act or Mid | Aorist Passive |
|---|---|---|---|
| ἀγαπάω, love | ἀγαπήσω | ἠγάπησα | ἠγαπήθην |
| αἴρω, lift up | ἀρῶ | ἦρα | ἤρθην |
| ἀκούω, hear | ἀκούσω | ἤκουσα | ἠκούσθην |
| ἀπέρχομαι, leave | ἀπελεύσομαι | ἀπῆλθον | —— |
| ἀποθνήσκω, die | ἀποθανοῦμαι | ἀπέθανον | —— |
| ἀποκρίνομαι, answer | —— | —— | ἀπεκρίθην |
| ἀποκτείνω, kill | ἀποκτενῶ | ἀπέκτεινα | ἀπεκτάνθην |
| ἀπόλλυμι, destroy | ἀπολέσω | ἀπώλησα | —— |
| ἀποστέλλω, send | ἀποστελῶ | ἀπέστειλα | ἀπεστάλην |
| ἀφίημι, forgive | ἀφησω | ἀφῆκα | ἀφέθην |
| βάλλω, throw | βαλῶ | ἔβαλον | ἐβλήθην |
| βλέπω, see | βλέψω | ἔβλεψα | |
| γεννάω, give birth | γεννήσω | ἐγέννησα | ἐγεννήθην |
| γίνομαι, become | γενήσομαι | ἐγενόμην | ἐγενήθην |
| γινώσκω, know | γνώσομαι | ἔγνων | ἐκνώσθην |
| γράφω, write | —— | ἔγραψα | ἐγράφην |
| διδάσκω, teach | διδάξω | ἐδίδαξα | ἐδιδάχθην |
| δίδωμι, give | δώσω | ἔδωκα | ἐδόθην |
| δουλεύω, serve | δουλεύσω | ἐδούλευσα | —— |
| δύναμαι, can | δυνήσομαι | —— | ἐδυνήθην |
| ἐγείρω, lift | ἐγερῶ | ἤγειρα | ἠγέρθην |
| εἰμί, am | ἔσομαι | —— | —— |
| ἔρχομαι, go | ἐλεύσομαι | ἦλθον | —— |
| ἐσθίω, eat | φάγομαι | ἔφαγον | —— |
| εὑρίσκω, find | εὑρήσω | εὗρον | εὑρέθην |
| ἔχω, have | ἕξω | ἔσχον | —— |
| ζάω, live | ζήσω | ἔζησα | —— |
| ζητέω, seek | ζητήσω | ἐζήτησα | —— |
| θέλω, desire | θελήσω | ἠθέλησα | —— |
| ἵστημι, stand | στήσω | ἔστησα, ἔστην | ἐστάθην |
| καλέω, call | καλέσω | ἐκάλεσα | ἐκλήθην |
| κρίνω, judge | κρινῶ | ἔκρινα | ἐκρίθην |
| λαλέω, speak | λαλήσω | ἐλάλησα | ἐλαλήθην |
| λαμβάνω, take | λήμψομαι | ἔλαβον | |
| λέγω, say | ἐρῶ | εἶπον | ἐρρέθην |
| μένω, remain | μενῶ | ἔμεινα | —— |
| ὁράω, see | ὄψομαι | εἶδον | ὤφθην |
| πίπτω, fall | πέσομαι | ἔπεσον, ἔπεσα | —— |

| | | | |
|---|---|---|---|
| πιστεύω, believe | πιστεύσω | ἐπίστευσα | ἐπιστεύθην |
| πληρόω, fill | πληρώσω | ἐπλήρωσα | ἐπληρώθην |
| ποιέω, do | ποιήσω | ἐποίησα | ἐποιήθην |
| πορεύομαι, go | πορεύσομαι | ———— | ἐπορυέθην |
| προσεύχομαι, pray | προσεύξομαι | προσηυξάμην | ———— |
| σώζω, save | σώσω | ἔσωσα | ἐσώθην |
| τίθημι, put | θήσω | ἔθηκα | ἐτέθην |

# INDEX

## 1

## 2

## A

## B

# J

# K

# L

# M

# U

# V

# W

# Y

**Richard B. Ramsay** (M.Div., D.Min., Westminster Theological Seminary; Th.M., Covenant Theological Seminary) is professor of Greek and apologetics at the distance education seminaries Faculty of Latin American Education in Theology (FLET) and Miami International Seminary (MINTS), as well as director of their online resources. He served in Chile for twenty-one years teaching Greek, New Testament, and apologetics and doing pastoral work. In addition to teaching and lecturing, Dr. Ramsay writes educational materials and designs Internet courses. He is the author of the Spanish titles *Cuán Bueno Debo Ser? A Su Imagen, Exploremos Génesis, Católicos y Protestantes, Integridad Intelectual, Certeza de la Fe*, and *Griego y Exégesis*. His English works include, *Am I Good Enough?* and *The Certainty of the Faith*. He is married to María Angélica from Chile, and they have two children, Nicolas and Melany.